BEFORE VIDEO

Recent Titles in
Contributions to the Study of Mass Media and Communications

BEFORE VIDEO

A History of the Non-Theatrical Film

ANTHONY SLIDE

*Contributions to the Study of Mass Media
and Communications, Number 35*

Greenwood Press
New York • Westport, Connecticut • London

Library of Congress Cataloging-in-Publication Data

Slide, Anthony.
    Before video : a history of the non-theatrical film / Anthony
Slide.
       p. cm.—(Contributions to the study of mass media and
communications, ISSN 0732–4456 ; no. 35)
    Includes bibliographical references (p.   ) and
index.
    ISBN 0–313–28045–2 (alk. paper)
    1. Industrial cinematography—History. I. Title. II. Series.
TR894.S55   1992
070.1′8—dc20   91–43367

British Library Cataloguing in Publication Data is available.

Library of Congress Catalog Card Number: 91–43367
ISBN: 0–313–28045–2
ISSN: 0732–4456

First published in 1992

Greenwood Press, 88 Post Road West, Westport, CT 06881
An imprint of Greenwood Publishing Group, Inc.

Printed in the United States of America

The paper used in this book complies with the
Permanent Paper Standard issued by the National
Information Standards Organization (Z39.48–1984).

10 9 8 7 6 5 4 3 2 1

Contents

Acknowledgments

Primary research for this book involved the reading of complete runs of *The Educational Screen, Business Screen Magazine, Film News, Sightlines,* and *Film Library Quarterly,* which cover the history of the non-theatrical and educational film genres from 1922 through the present. For access to these and other research materials, I am grateful to the Margaret Herrick Library of the Academy of Motion Picture Arts and Sciences, the Louis B. Mayer Library of the American Film Institute, the Los Angeles Central Library, and the Doheny Memorial Library of the University of Southern California.

I would also like to thank Rudy Behlmer, Q. David Bowers, the Council on International Nontheatrical Events (Joy Parisi), Layne Dreben, Robert Gitt, Hal Guthrie, Ron Hall, Pat and Steve Hanson, Kit Parker, Timothy M. Rogers (Chairman of the Division of Cinema at Bob Jones University), and Noel Van Gorden (Chief of the Burton Historical Collection at the Detroit Public Library). At Greenwood Press, I would like to thank Marilyn Brownstein, Arlene Belzer, and, this time also, Robert Hagelstein.

For his enthusiasm and help, I am particularly grateful to Thomas W. Hope, Chairman of Hope Reports, Inc.

Research materials gathered in the preparation of this volume have been deposited with the Popular Culture Library at Bowling Green State University.

Introduction

In 1975, Sony introduced the first commercially viable home videotape system, Betamax. A year later, another Japanese company, JVC, came out with what was to become the most popular of home videotape processes, the VHS or Video Home System. By 1984, it was reported that 15.8 percent of U.S. households had at least one videocassette recorder (or VCR). VCR sales in the mid-1980s topped one million a month, until as of May 1, 1990, more than 70 percent of U.S. households had videocassette recorders.[1]

The videotape revolution, as it came to be known, totally changed the manner in which Americans entertained themselves. The moviegoing experience began to fade as former theatregoers found it cheaper, more convenient, and often less harrowing to rent and sometimes purchase videotapes of their favorite films. Television programming could be recorded on tape for later viewing or reviewing. The operation of a videotape recorder/player was as simple as the use of any kitchen appliance, making access to videotape immediate for even the most technically uneducated.

Videotape provided a feeling of immediacy that film could not offer. With the latter medium, the viewer was simply that—an outsider looking in. Thanks to video, the viewer was offered the feeling of being there, a sense of intimacy and participation. As librarian Cliff Ehlinger wrote in *Sightlines*, "This growth in the videotape format has been fueled

by a more sophisticated public—a public which has come to rely on the
video image as a primary source of entertainment and information. We
are caught in a wave of technology which has forced all of us to expect
instant feedback, useable and improving visual/audio quality, ease of
operation and lower cost."[2]

Despite the advent of videotape, commercial movie houses have survived. The same is not true of the non-commercial, non-35mm film
industry. The non-theatrical film field was the worst hit by the video
revolution. While the non-theatrical film industry continues to exist in
a very limited form, the impact of videotape has been both dramatic
and, ultimately, devastating for it.

From an economic viewpoint, there is little similarity between non-
theatrical and videotape revenues. In 1973, the total non-theatrical film
rentals in the United States amounted to a mere $125 million. Revenues
from the video rental of a single Hollywood feature film can top $100
million. As of 1990, *Batman* had earned $179.4 million and *Who Framed
Roger Rabbit?* $111.7 million. Some films have grossed more in home
video rentals than in the boxoffice returns from their theatrical release.

In order to survive, institutions and publications long devoted to the
non-theatrical film were forced to change either their names or their
outlooks—or both. Videotape was first shown at the non-theatrical film's
best-known outlet, the American Film Festival, in 1979. That same year,
the National Video Clearinghouse was created to service the needs of
video software users. In 1986, the American Film Festival changed its
name to the American Film & Video Festival; and the following year its
organizer, the Educational Film Library Association, changed its name
to the American Film & Video Association. As early as 1975, *Booklist*,
published by the American Library Association, began reviewing video
cassettes; two years later, *Film Library Quarterly* also introduced reviews
of video releases. The latter publication, first published in winter 1967–
1968 by the Film Library Information Council, was forced to cease publication in 1984, with Volume XVII, Nos. 2, 3, and 4, and merged with
Sightlines. The following year, R. R. Bowker published the eighth and
last edition of James Limbacher's *Feature Films on 8mm and 16mm* under
the title of *Feature Films: A Directory on Feature Films on 16mm and Videotape
Available for Rental, Sale, and Lease.*

The demise of the non-theatrical film seems an appropriate time for
a history of the genre, which is, unfortunately, not an easy one to define.
At its most basic, the non-theatrical film is a term used to describe films
not screened in commercial venues (i.e., theatres), but in homes, offices,
libraries, institutions, and other non-theatrical sites.

In his important early study, *The Informational Film*, John Mercer has
argued that the non-theatrical film can be divided into three categories:
films in the psychomotor domain (which teach a skill), films in the

cognitive domain (which record and inform), and films in the affective domain (which persuade or propagandize).[3] While not disagreeing with Mercer, I would argue that the non-theatrical film can better, and more simply, be subdivided into two major categories. The term can be utilized to describe the presentation of Hollywood- (or commercially) produced features and short subjects in a format other than 35mm and in a non-theatre setting. It can also be used to describe films specifically produced for non-theatrical use, primarily to educate or inform audiences, often sponsored by companies with an interest in the subject matter. Films in this category can also be called sponsored or industrial films. Non-theatrical film is generally 16mm, but to a lesser extent it can be 8mm or even an obscure and defunct film gauge such as 17.5mm or 28mm. Because such gauges are smaller than standard 35mm film, they are sometimes described as "substandard," a term that unfortunately and unintentionally carries a derogatory connotation.

Prior to the introduction of 16mm film stock, sponsored or industrial films were produced in 35mm. However, with the introduction of 16mm film, the genre gained prominence as an industry in its own right. In the mid-1930s, George H. Sewell, chairman of the British Institute of Amateur Cinematographers, commented, "In the cinema film, you have a medium which is at once attractive and interesting; a powerful educator and propagandist. Combine these things in the form known as sub-standard film and you have them in a form which will give the widest scope and which is at the same time supremely safe and supremely easy to use."[4]

J. G. Capstaff of the Eastman Kodak Research Laboratories began experimenting with 16mm film between 1915 and 1920. The research was hindered by the First World War, but by 1920 Capstaff had developed both a 16mm camera and projector. Dr. C.E.K. Mees, director of the Kodak Research Laboratories, supervised the manufacture of the first 16mm black-and-white film stock (which was reversal rather than negative film) on January 8, 1923. On July 5, 1923, the new "Ciné-Kodak" 16mm equipment was advertised in the *New York Times* and the *New York Tribune*. Also in 1923, 16mm cameras and projectors were introduced by two companies, the Victor Animatograph Corporation (with its "Victor" model) and Bell & Howell (with the "Filmo").

Experiments with 16mm sound film began in 1927, and three years later Eastman Kodak developed what was to become the standard 16mm sound film, with a row of perforations down one side and with the other side available for the soundtrack. The early 35mm sound system Vitaphone had utilized sound-on-discs, and the first 16mm sound films adopted a similar system. The first specially designed and constructed 16mm sound projector was introduced by the Victor Animatograph Corporation in December 1930, with the sound-on-disc records being placed in a vertical rather than the usual horizontal position. The first 16mm sound-on-film projector was introduced by RCA in 1932; it was named the Junior Portable to avoid confusion with a 35mm portable projector the company had brought out the previous year. In 1935, RCA developed a 16mm sound camera.

Other companies quickly marketed 16mm sound-on-film projectors, beginning with the Filmosound introduced by Bell & Howell in 1933. The following year, DeVry (which had introduced a 16mm silent projector in 1927) and Ampro Corporation of Chicago came out with their first 16mm sound projectors.

One important aspect of 16mm film stock was that it was cellulose acetate rather than nitrate based, as was 35mm film stock prior to 1950, and therefore basically non-flammable. Unlike 35mm nitrate film, 16mm was considered not to be a fire hazard and therefore to be safe for use in the home, classroom, church, and other non-theatrical settings. The selection of the 16mm gauge and the insistence that it should be available only on safety film were two major decisions by Eastman Kodak. The choice of a gauge 16mm in width was quite deliberate in that it precluded the splitting of 35mm film stock.[5]

Other early, non-35mm film gauges that preceded 16mm were generally also safety based. In the United States, the earliest was 22mm film, utilizing three rows of pictures with perforations between each, which was developed in 1912 by Thomas A. Edison, Inc., for use on the Edison Home Kinetoscope. However, the equipment, as its name implies, was intended primarily for home use and was not a viable alternative to 35mm in the early non-theatrical market developing in the first two decades of the twentieth century.

NOTES

1. See "VCR Penetration Breaks 70% Barrier," *Variety*, May 16, 1990, p. 35; "VCR Sales Hit Fast-Forward in '90," *Variety*, March 28, 1990, p. 39; and "VCR and Paycable Penetration," *Variety*, September 13, 1989, p. 66.

2. Cliff Ehlinger, "Video and Film Libraries Herald a New Era," *Sightlines*, vol. XXII, no. 1 (Winter 1988/89), p. 14.

3. John Mercer, *The Informational Film* (Champaign, Ill.: Stipes Publishing Company, 1981), p. 3.

4. George H. Sewell, *Commercial Cinematography* (London: Sir Isaac Pitman & Sons, n.d.), p. 1.

5. A good general history of the 16mm film is provided in Glenn E. Matthews and Raife G. Tarkington, "Early History of Amateur Motion-Picture Film," *Journal of SMPTE*, vol. LXIV, no. 3 (March 1955), pp. 105–16.

ONE

Origins

The first American public screenings of motion pictures took place in vaudeville houses. The first Edison productions were screened at Koster and Bial's Music Hall in April 1896; the Lumière films shown at Keith's Union Square Theatre in July of the same year were followed by the American Biograph program at Hammerstein's Olympia Theatre in October 1896. All were part of a regular vaudeville bill, and audiences had not paid specifically to view the new novelty of the motion picture. In that sense, it might be argued that the first film presentations in the United States were non-theatrical.

Those first films consisted of waves breaking on the shore, the arrival of the mail train, a parade of soldiers, the Upper Rapids of Niagara, scenes at London's Hyde Park, and similar items. All could be classified as educational or informational in content and, yet again, were the first examples of non-theatrical filmmaking.

Their producers might argue that these films were nothing of the sort, being either experimental or commercial ventures. The one filmmaker who would disagree is Thomas Alva Edison, the man whose name is most closely associated (in name if not in deed) with the invention of the motion picture and the man who perceived film not as a commercial venture but as an educational tool. Many of Edison's views on education are considered eccentric at best; he saw no value in learning a dead language such as Latin or a worthless mathematical subject such as algebra, but he did believe in the importance of America's youth learning a trade, which could be more readily accomplished through the use of the motion picture. Writing in his diary in 1925, Edison pondered, "Maybe I'm wrong, but I should say that in ten years textbooks as the principal medium of teaching will be obsolete as the horse and carriage are now. I believe that in the next ten years visual education—the imparting of extant information through the motion picture camera—will be a matter of course in all of our schools. The printed lesson will be largely supplemental—not paramount."

Edison's view of the motion picture as an educational medium was a long-held one. In a 1913 interview, he explained,

> The motion picture is the great educator of the poorer people. It incites their imagination by bringing the whole world before their eyes. It sets spectators thinking and raises their standard of living. . . .
>
> Books will soon be obsolete in the public schools. Scholars will be instructed through the eye. It is possible to teach every branch of human knowledge with the motion picture. Our school system will be completely changed inside of ten years.
>
> We have been working for some time on the school pictures. We have been studying and reproducing the life of the fly, mosquito, silk weaving moth, brown moth, gypsy moth, butterflies, scale and various other insects, as well as chemical crystallization. It proves conclusively the worth of motion pictures in chemistry, physics and other branches of study, making the scientific truths, difficult to understand from text books, plain and clear to children.[1]

Of the short films copyrighted as paper prints by the Thomas A. Edison Company between 1894 and 1912, a sizeable number are actuality subjects, which might well be classified as educational. Typical examples are *Government House at Hong Kong* (1898), *Picking Oranges* (1898), *Watermelon Contest* (1900), *Tobogganing in Canada* (1902), *Electrocuting an Elephant* (1903), *Lake Lucerne, Switzerland* (1903), *Shearing a Donkey in Egypt* (1903), and *Ice Skating in Central Park, N.Y.* (1904).

The Thomas A. Edison Company also produced perhaps the earliest advertising film, for Admiral Cigarettes, in 1897. Other advertising subjects produced by a rival company, the American Mutoscope and Biograph, include *The Gold Dust Twins* (1903, for Gold Dust Scouring Powder), *Mellin's Foods* (1904), *Shredded Wheat Biscuit* (1904), and *Chauncey Explains* (1905, for Equitable Life).

An early rival but later colleague of Edison was George Kleine (1864–1931), who was to distribute many of the Edison productions. In 1910, he published one of the first catalogs of non-theatrical films, and he was again active in the non-theatrical field in the early 1920s. In 1922, Kleine boasted that he had twenty-two universities around the United States distributing his films. Eight years later, Kleine wrote to Edison, "While the financial side is hardly interesting, as the earnings no more than cover the modest expenses of handling, there are many interesting angles to this work, which I look upon from a nonprofit standpoint as experimental in the nontheatrical field."[2]

Another friend of Edison, Henry Ford, was also a pioneer in the development of non-theatrical film. Recognizing the advertising potential of film, Ford created a motion picture department within his company in 1914. His company produced two weekly series, *Ford Animated Weekly* (1914–1921) and *Ford Educational Weekly* (1916–1925), which were not shown, as were newsreels, in commercial theatres, but rather were offered at no charge to institutions such as the YMCA. Additionally, Ford produced a multitude of short subjects. The content of these and the weekly series did not generally relate to either Ford or his company but rather included subjects as varied as cities and countries, President Woodrow Wilson, sporting events, agriculture, personalities of the day, industry, nature studies, and even a handful of cartoons.[3]

As early as 1908, *Bohemian Magazine* reported:

> In several of the larger cities educational and philanthropic institutions have adopted the moving-picture plan of instruction and entertainment; at least two of the big railroad systems have announced their intention to resort to these methods of inducing colonization through their industrial departments, and the leading officials of the Salvation Army are so deeply interested in the attempt to make the moving picture an important feature at religious meetings that they are now engaged in manufacturing several large and very striking films for their own use.
>
> So far as the regular manufacturers are concerned, they are now beginning to realize the possibilities offered in the educational field, and nearly all the most progressive houses are now exerting a certain portion of their efforts in this direction.[4]

Between 1910 and 1920, many hundreds of films were released annually in the United States, screened commercially, and yet they were completely educational in nature. One typical example is Pathé's *The Analysis of Motion*, released on April 11, 1913, which used slow motion photography to show the formation of drops of water, the trajectory of a bullet, and a jet of water. The reviewer in the *New York Dramatic Mirror* (March 26, 1913) called the production "the first really practical film— the initial step into an educational film [field] the size of which a present day mind cannot grasp."

Travelogs, usually accompanied by informational lectures, have survived to the present as one of the few areas of non-theatrical film relatively untouched by video. They have their origins in the work of Burton Holmes and Lyman Howe, two traveling showmen who initially did not distribute their productions in the usual fashion but accompanied them around the country commenting in person on the films and often introducing the new medium to audiences far removed from commercial movie theatres or nickelodeons. Based in Chicago, Burton Holmes began film production in 1897, followed in 1905 by H. Lyman Howe, working out of Wilkes-Barre, Pennsylvania. "My business was founded and is dependent upon educational films. They are the very things that made my success," commented Howe in 1913.[5] Howe was not able to make the transition from traveling showman to non-theatrical producer/distributor, but Holmes did. His company survived in one form or another well into the 1980s.

Another who specialized in travel films early in the cinema's evolution was New York–based Dwight L. Elmendorf, active as early as 1898, following in the tradition of Henry Northrop and Alexander Black, who presented a combination of travel films and lantern slides. An early novelty entertainment that might well be classified as non-theatrical was Hale's Tours and Scenes of the World, first opened by George C. Hale at the Electric Park, Kansas City, in May 1905 and popular at various locations throughout the United States for the next five years or so. The audience was treated as passengers boarding a train-like theatre and viewing films back-projected at the carriage's front.

Hale's Tours and Scenes of the World was later relegated to the fairground and had disappeared by 1912, but many travel films had more prestigious presentations. Beginning on February 7, 1913, Beverly B. Dobbs' feature on Alaska and Siberia, *Atop the World in Motion*, was screened at New York's Carnegie Hall.

There were, however, limitations on the locations at which sponsored, industrial, or informational films might be screened. The films might fall into the non-theatrical genre, but their presentations were, of necessity, theatrical. Certainly portable projection equipment was readily available, and as early as 1907 Sears, Roebuck & Company published a separate catalog of *Motion Picture Machines, Magic Lanterns and Stereopticons, Slides, Films and Supplies* available to customers; but the film was highly inflammable nitrate stock, undoubtably dangerous if shown at unlicensed premises and/or with unprofessional operators handling the projection. Although 35mm safety film was introduced by Eastman Kodak as early as 1907, it was brittle and subject to shrinkage and was generally disregarded for day-to-day commercial use.

Nicholas Power, one of the most prominent early manufacturers of projection equipment, active from the 1890s onward, explained in 1913, "When we consider the motion picture in the home, we must consider the element of safety from the standpoint of the law. Our laws insist upon certain requirements, such as a competent licensed operator. Then there is the question of insurance. But I am confident that the machine can be absolutely safe."[6]

Safe or otherwise, group screenings of educational or informational films were limited to movie houses and, by 1915–1920, to a handful of school sites. The advocacy for educational use of films was strong. In 1914, one school superintendent noted, "The motion picture multiplies the advantages of the ordinary picture a thousandfold. It is the means of the greatest possibilities in the way of information. Its benefits are incalculable. It may be regarded as a great educational lever whereby the very great portion of our present-day schoolroom work may be lifted out of the shadows of the valley of the abstract into the clear sunlight of human interest."[7]

Outside restraints were to limit educational use of the motion picture, but its importance to industry in self-promotion and advertising was very obvious to many companies. In 1912, the Essanay Film Manufacturing Company produced *Back to the Old Farm*, with sponsorship by the International Harvester Company. The following year, C. W. Post produced *The Making of Pure Foods at Battle Creek*.[8] Within two years more than a dozen companies had commenced film sponsorship, including such prominent names as the Shredded Wheat Company, the National Cash Register Company, Marshall Field and Company, the Commonwealth Edison Company, the American Hoist and Derrick Company, the Pacific Coast Borax Company, and the Du Pont Powder Company.

In 1912, the New Rochelle–based Thanhouser Film Corporation produced *An American in the Making*, starring Harry Benham, Ethyle Cooke, and Leland Benham and released on April 22, 1913. *An American in the Making* was shot at Ellis Island; at the Gary, Indiana, works of the U.S. Steel Corporation; and at the National Tube Works in Lorain, Ohio. Although financed by U.S. Steel, the film was promoted as produced to aid the work of the National Social Betterment Association.

In an address on January 27, 1914, before the New York Theatre Club (as reported in the February 14, 1914, issue of *Reel Life*), Thanhouser's president C. J. Hite discussed the film and presented his view on the educational film in general:

> About a year ago the United States Steel Corporation came to us and requested us to prepare a story in moving picture form, with the idea of circulating the same through our theatres, which would show the human side of this great company. They wanted to convey to the public in general that they had a heart; that they were also interested in the education, health and safety of their employees. It resulted in the following story.
>
> A brother in America writes to Bela in Poland that he has a job for him. He arrives at Ellis Island, is tagged to Gary, Indiana, the home of the steel trust, and there met his brother, who shows him this wonderful plant and

had him lined up for a job, where he starts in on the commonest kind of jobs, is promoted from one position to another until it brings him in contact with all the dangerous mechanical devices in places where his life is jeopardized, but at each turn in this road of progress through the plant where his life is endangered a safety signal is displayed, called his attention to the danger of injury. He attends night school, and we complete the story of our hero with respect to the U.S. Steel Corporation by marrying him happily to his little American night school teacher, with a scene in their cottage at the table with their family.

At the present time the Department of Labor is working on a series of motion pictures which are to be an argument intended to educate and impress both capital and labor with the folly of strikes. This is only one of the great problems of vital interest to humanity in which motion pictures may be made a great factor in bringing contentment and happiness to all races. Educational institutions, after having realized its great values, are rapidly adopting the objective kinetic method of training. Thus the method will be universally adopted, sciences can be more easily propounded and since it is a universal language, arguments between factions, people and nations can be discussed and decided on the screen; thus tending to avert and possibly averting wars, thus improving and spreading civilization in a manner which will raise the standard of all races.

Trade papers reviewing *An American in the Making* made no reference to its sponsorship by U.S. Steel, except to note the use of the corporation's facility. *The Moving Picture World* (May 3, 1913) wrote, "Such a film as this makes an interesting novelty and distributes valuable information concerning industrial matters." If nothing else, *An American in the Making* marked the beginning of U.S. Steel's long involvement with industrial films. By 1969, it had more than fifty films in distribution from its centers in Birmingham, Chicago, New York, Pittsburgh, and San Francisco, seen at that time by a total audience of more than twenty million.[9]

To meet the needs of sponsors such as the U.S. Steel Corporation, an industrial film industry was established outside of the commercial/theatrical industry. Centered on Chicago rather than Hollywood, it was to create its own personalities and venerate companies such as the Jam Handy Organization or Wilding Picture Productions in much the same way that M-G-M or Warner Bros. were respected for the quality of their productions. It was an industry with its own trade papers, its own trade organizations, and even its own award ceremonies.

Industry might have continued to use the major commercial producers of the day, but in a typically shortsighted move this practice was halted by the Motion Picture Patents Company, representing the interests of the major licensed production houses. The situation came to a head in 1910, when the Vitagraph Company produced a short subject titled *Dolly and Jim in Chew-Chew Land*. A rival producer, the Selig Polyscope Company, complained that the film was nothing more than an advertising short and that it should not be released as part of the general program, blatant advertising films being unpopular with audiences and "injurous to the business of motion picture exhibitors."[10] As a result of Selig's complaints, the member producing companies of the Motion Picture Patents Company agreed not to accept compensation for advertising products in their films; if they did, such compensation had to be shared with all the other companies. Little impetus remained to continue a practice that would only provide financial benefit to one's rivals.

In May 1910, the Selig Polyscope Company pressed members of the Motion Picture Patents Company not to allow its films to be screened in theatres that showed advertising films from other sources, pointing out that Anheuser Busch had apparently produced such films and was making them available to exhibitors at no rental charge. In a further blow to a relationship between the film industry and outside commercial concerns, in June 1910, the Motion Picture Patents Company rejected a proposal from Procter & Gamble that patrons of movie houses be allowed to exchange soap wrappers for admission tickets with the soap company picking up the tab.

As with most of the decisions of the Motion Picture Patents Company—for example, it was opposed to feature-length production—the negativity toward advertising was shortsighted. It ignored totally a 1912 report by the U.S. Department of Commerce that pointed out that American films were a major source of publicity for American products, estimating that every foot of film exported sold a dollar's worth of American goods. The public was willing to accept a certain proportion of industrial films in theatrical programming, if the films were entertaining or sufficiently informative to hold one's attention. Commenting on two 1914 sponsored films, *The Record of Thrift* from the American Bankers' Association and *The Price of Thoughtlessness* (which demonstrated the dangers to children of playing in the streets and the correct methods of boarding and alighting from trolley cars) from the National Safety-First Societies, the *New York Dramatic Mirror* editorialized, "Pictures telling a story solely for the purpose of driving home a certain moral are at present scarce, but there is every indication that they will become more and more popular, for the picture patron has been found perfectly willing to be taught a lesson by way of the screen."[11]

It could be argued that the non-theatrical film has its origins in the seventeenth century, when Thommoso Campanella argued that all learning must take place through the senses and thus earned for himself the title of father of audiovisual education. However, in a rambling yet extraordinarily detailed history of the non-theatrical film, published from 1938 through 1944 in the pages of *The Educational Screen*, Arthur Edwin Krows dates 1910 as the year in which the non-theatrical film came into

existence.[12] His choice of that year is based on the aforementioned activities of the Motion Picture Patents Company, the recognition by the
trade paper *The Moving Picture World* of the value of film in church work,
the advocacy of films in the classroom by the New York City school
superintendent, and, perhaps most important of all, the establishment
of what is generally believed to be the first industrial film company in
the United States, Raths-Seavolt Film Manufacturing Company.

The company was founded in February 1910 in St. Paul, Minnesota,
by Otto N. Raths and Edward Seavolt, primarily to produce local newsreels for the city's Gaiety Theatre and promotional shorts for the Great
Northern Railway. Charles E. Bell was the company's cinematographer.
In 1921, W. R. Mills acquired partial ownership of the company, and it
was renamed Raths, Mills & Bell; four years later Reid H. Ray (a writer
of industrial films) took over the management, which adopted the company's best-known name, Ray-Bell Films, Inc. With Bell's retirement in
July 1947, a further name change to Reid H. Ray Industries took place.
The company was sold in 1975 to Jim Zitek of Minneapolis-based Zitek
& Associates.

The St. Paul location of Raths-Seavolt illustrates that the non-theatrical
film industry was not based in the then two centers of film production,
New York and Los Angeles. It did not need a central core of players as
did the theatrical industry, nor did it require an everchanging group of
directors, cinematographers, and other technicians. Scripts would often
be provided by the advertising departments of the sponsors; and if not,
they could be written in-house or on commission from anywhere in the
country. Almost the only requirement for a non-theatrical company was
a neighboring film laboratory, and many companies eventually built their
own, handling not only in-house developing and printing but also turning a steady profit for their owners through acceptance of outside work.

In 1912, Ernest S. Carpenter opened the Escar Motion Picture Service
in Cleveland, Ohio. Joseph De Frenes established the De Frenes Company in Philadelphia in 1916. The Educational Film Bureau was created
by two former teachers named Lincoln and Parker in 1914 in Worcester,
Massachusetts (which was later to be home to the Worcester Film Corporation). The Reserve Photo Plays Company was formed in Cleveland
in 1916; its first production, for the General Electric Company, was *Flame
Eternal, a Drama of Light and Love*. In 1915, cinematographer Harry F.
Green organized the Ovaca Motion Picture Corporation in Nashville.
The Jamieson Film Company was founded in Dallas in 1916. In 1914,
Norman E. Wilding (1891–1947), a traveling salesman for lighting fix-
tures, founded Wilding Picture Productions. Incorporated in 1927, it
grew to be one of the country's largest non-theatrical film production
houses, with offices, as of 1947, in Chicago, Detroit, Cleveland, New
York, and Hollywood.

Dozens of companies chose Chicago as their home base, while among the many producers in New York were the Home Feature Film Company, founded in 1914 by Norman R. Buckley and M. F. Joliffe, and the William J. Ganz Company formed in 1919. Also in New York, Camilla Dunworth established the Films of Business Corporation in December 1917; one of its first productions was *One of the Departments of a Great Industry* for the H. J. Heinz Company.

Organizations to represent the interests of both producers and sponsors of industrial films were created as quickly as the companies that belonged to them. In 1913, the Bureau of Commercial Economics was founded as "an association of leading institutions, manufacturers, producers and transportation lines in this country and abroad, to engage in disseminating industrial and vocational information by the graphic method of motion pictures, upon the commendation of the leading educators of the country."[13] The Bureau was co-founded by Dr. Frances Holley and Anita M. Boggs, and the latter became director upon Holley's death in December 1923. The Screen Advertisers' Association, which held its first meeting in Chicago in 1914, was headed by a national committee of three: W. R. (Watterson) Rothacker, Charles Stark, and J. Alexander Leggett. The last operated his own advertising agency in New York and produced films for clients including AT&T.

The sales force of American industry had fully endorsed the use of motion pictures by 1914. The *New York Dramatic Mirror* reported:

The progressive up-to-the-minute salesman no longer worries about excess baggage rates, likewise he is freed from everlasting packing and unpacking unwieldly sample trunks and cases at every stopping point in his itinerary; also the uncertainty of reserving sample rooms conforming to his needs. These and attendant trials and tribulations have been eliminated from his path of progress. Instead, he sallies forth modernly equipped with a small compact carrying case containing one or more reels of motion pictures, a projecting machine and light attachments; the complete outfit not weighing over fifty pounds; stepping into a would-be customer's office, he is readily granted the privilege of demonstrating his firm's product through the entertaining medium of motion photography. His stage is a bare wall or wide window space, a darkened room and a light socket. In a few minutes' time he has transformed the merchant's drab little quarters into a bijou theater; while his host sits comfortably back in a swivel chair leisurely puffing an after-dinner cigar. Perfectly wonderful, he ejaculates in mild astonishment, never believed such things were possible; surely this is an age of miracles, and so on, that chatter keeps up until the last foot of film is run and the convinced prospect obligingly confers the best order possible on the wily magician. Such are the methods spelling success, integrity, progress, and advancement.[14]

Within a few years, it was not even necessary for the salesman to carry all the appropriate films with him or to await freight delivery. The ease and speed by which traveling salesmen could obtain films was vastly improved as of January 1, 1917, when new regulations made it possible to ship films via parcel post. The postal service was not to provide another such boost for the non-theatrical film market until July 20, 1953, when President Eisenhower signed into law a bill giving educational films the same fourth-class mailing privileges as books.

Some production companies in the early years were created to specialize in one field, only to become prominent later as non-theatrical concerns. Such an organization was Bray Studios, Inc., established in New York in 1914 by John Randolph Bray (1879–1978), the son of a Methodist minister and a former cartoonist on the staff of the *Detroit News*. The company was to produce cartoon shorts utilizing a patented process developed by Bray and Earl Hurd. The cartoons remained popular through the early 1930s; but in 1915 Bray expanded into production of industrial and educational shorts, and these ultimately were the most profitable of the company's activities.

During the First World War, Bray produced training films for the U.S. Army, utilizing animation techniques developed by his mechanical draftsman, J. F. Leventhal. In 1921, Bray was perhaps the first American non-theatrical producer to expand into the foreign market, helping to create the Okomoto Co. in Japan. Three years later, Leventhal produced a series of twelve short subjects on communicable diseases and personal hygiene titled "The Science of Life," produced in cooperation with the U.S. Public Health Service.

Bray Studios, Inc., prospered and survived not because of its cartoons but because it had taken the initiative in combining animation with non-theatrical production, eventually finding the latter most economically viable. As Leonard Maltin has written in his history of the animated film *Of Mice and Men*,

> Bray's biggest move was into the field of instructional film. J. F. Leventhal impressed Bray with his realistic animation, and this set the producer onto a new course, that of pioneering the largely untapped educational film market. Bray developed the prototype for filmstrips and filmstrip projectors; when 16mm safety film was introduced, he released the entire backlog of live-action footage from his Paramount (and later Goldwyn) Pictographs with great success. Bray's educational films division prospered long after the theatrical business failed, and the studio bearing his name is still going strong.[15]

Another company that followed much the same scenario as Bray's was the Eastern Film Corporation, founded in 1915 by Frederick S. Peck and active through the mid-1930s. It was involved in the production and distribution of a number of comedy short series—"Sparkle Comedies," "Pokes and Jabs," and "Finn and Haddie"—but by 1915–1920 was primarily involved in the production subjects for DuPont, the American Wallpaper Association, the Public Service Corporation of New Jersey, the American Society for the Control of Cancer, the National Board of Fire Underwriters, the Glens Falls Insurance Company, and the Aetna Fire Insurance Company. Eastern's production manager was Arch Heath, who was later to enjoy a career in Hollywood as a "B" picture director, and the company also employed two cameramen who became prominent in the theatrical film industry, W. Howard Green and Harry Stradling.

A company that took the opposite route to Bray and Eastern, beginning as a non-theatrical producer and later becoming a well-known name in the Hollywood film community, was the Educational Films Corporation. The company was founded in New York in May 1915 by E. W. (Earle Woolridge) Hammons (1882–1962) with an initial investment of $5,800. Early in its operation, Educational was the recipient of an investment of $30,000 from a wealthy businessman named George A. Skinner, who was later to become treasurer of the Payne Fund and to organize the Motion Picture Research Council. Skinner was appointed Educational's president and encouraged the company's production of educational subjects such as its first release, a three-reel short titled *When the Mountains Call*, produced by Robert Bruce and photographed in the Cascade Mountains of Washington State.

The company's logo, a rendition of Aladdin's lamp, was suggested by Mrs. Catherine Carter and executed by Carl Heck. The lamp and a later slogan, "The Spice of the Program," became familiar to theatrical moviegoers beginning in the 1920s. The change in policy at Educational after Skinner left the company in 1917 was not immediate. For example, in the 1918–1919 season, Educational produced at least five series of educational subjects, Robert C. Bruce's *Scenics of Adventure in the Northwest*, Raymond L. Ditmars' *The Living Book of Nature*, George D. Wright's *Mexico Today*, Dwight L. Elmendorf's foreign travel films, and E. M. Newman's Far East films.

Reorganized in 1927 as Educational Pictures, Inc., the company produced comedy shorts featuring Lloyd Hamilton, Lupino Lane, and others; in the 1930s it was responsible for some of the first screen comedies of Danny Kaye and Bert Lahr. After Educational declared bankruptcy in 1940, E. W. Hammons ended his career back in the non-theatrical film industry. Appointed president of Ross Federal Service in 1945, he was responsible for the creation of a new 16mm films division.

Without question the most familiar name in industrial film production is the Jam Handy Organization, Inc.; its first predecessor company was founded in 1910 by Jamison Handy and Herbert Kaufman. (The latter wrote inspirational articles for the *Chicago Tribune* and its syndicate.) The son of the publicity director for the 1893 World's Columbian Exposition, Jamison (Jam) Handy began his adult life as an assistant in the editorial and advertising departments of the *Chicago Tribune*. Undoubtedly his father's and his own career origins helped Handy develop an interest in communications. His and Kaufman's first client, in 1911, was the National Cash Register Company. But the first project, although involving visual communication, was not a motion picture; and it is quite possible that Jam Handy did not make his first film for the National Cash Register Company until 1920.

The National Cash Register Company and its president John Patterson were well aware of the value of visual images for instructional purposes. Patterson believed strongly that people thought in visual terms, and he would even use matchstick men on his desk to get over a point to colleagues. Patterson had built up a library of 20,000 magic lantern slides, which were a little more professional than his matchstick men. Slides were the predecessors of motion pictures in the audiovisual field, and the transition from one to the other was natural. In fact, magic lantern slides are considered the obvious precursor to the theatrical motion picture. Magic lanternists in the Victorian era would present slides as entertainment, using dissolves and similar devices to present a sense of movement.

"Our first job at National Cash Register was to inform and enthuse sales people, first with 'turnover' charts, which we now call flip-charts," recalled Handy in 1971. "And we also started to train NCR service mechanics with outlines of gears and levers on the charts. John Patterson had one basic idea on those charts which is that no sheet of paper, no matter how big you make it, is big enough for more than one idea."[16]

Handy had the foresight to realize that in order to grow the company would need, in its early years, not only to produce films but also to distribute or syndicate them to theatres. Clients did not wish to pay for productions that might be denied an audience; and the exhibition of industrial films has been of constant, and continuing, concern to both producers and sponsors. Handy recalled,

> Household appliances and new kitchen conveniences were just coming into popularity in the years before World War I. They were elementary in those days, but people got into trouble even with can openers. They needed at least to know which end was the handle. Women and men, too, were really interested in that stuff. The theatres had felt there was no entertainment value or audience interest in anything but love, murder, mystery and crime. But we sold the idea that, after all, the people who are coming to theatres are the same people who read newspapers and they are interested in the news. So we succeeded in putting facts in the theatres, along with the fiction.[17]

John Patterson's belief in visual aids was important to Handy's growth, as was the support of Richard H. Grant, president of the Chevrolet Motor Company. Through Grant's influence, Handy began to produce films for General Motors and commenced the move of his company to its logical home in Detroit, while continuing to produce slide presentations in Chicago.

According to Arthur Edwin Krows, "It was Jim Handy's idea from the beginning to supply a complete motion picture service; so his workers not only variously wrote scenarios and produced pictures but they negotiated print sales, inspected and repaired reels in use, and actually put on shows. They sold projectors, too."[18]

For the first dozen or so years of its existence, the Jam Handy Organization was headquartered in Chicago and known under a variety of names, including the Newspapers Film Corporation. The name of Jam Handy Picture Service, adopted in the 1920s, became the only name by which the organization was known as of 1929. The following year, Jam Handy relocated completely to Detroit, occupying a converted church on East Grand Boulevard, which was claimed to be the first talking-picture studio exclusively for industrial filmmaking. That same year, the company boasted it had produced the first musical comedy at a business convention for the Coca-Cola Company; and in 1937, it produced the first Technicolor industrial film, *Refreshment through the Years*, also for the Coca-Cola Company.

Coca-Cola was but one of Jam Handy's major clients in the 1930s. Others were General Motors, the Curtis Publishing Company, Johns-Manville, the Bankers Trust Company, the General Electric Company, and Cantrell & Cochrane, Ltd.

The changeover from film to video in the 1970s and 1980s marked the decline of the Jam Handy Organization. As it wound down operations, various divisions were sold off. In 1988, it moved to the northern Detroit suburb of Royal Oak and later that same year went out of business. Jamison Handy died on November 3, 1983. The year before his death, he was featured in television commercials for the summer Olympic games as the only living person to have won gold medals for swimming in two Olympic games eight years apart.

America's entry into the First World War provided a new non-theatrical outlet—the U.S. armed forces in need of motion pictures for both relaxation and edification. In order to approve films for military screenings, the U.S. government helped create the Community Motion Picture Bureau, headed by Warren Dunham Foster. The bureau eventually handled the film servicing not only for American troops but also, on a partial basis, for those from the United Kingdom, Canada, Australia, France, and New Zealand. The physical handling of the films was supervised by Henry Bollman, and the censorship of the productions was undertaken by Foster's mother Edith Dunham Foster. According to Arthur Edwin Krows:

> Most of Mrs. Foster's editorial work was to sit in judgment on the newly-received films, cutting out all the pretty ladies, drinking scenes, naughty titles and similar slips which might demoralize the soldiers in the trenches. Reporting to her, for her guidance, were division workers of the Bureau and of the Y.M.C.A., stationed at many strategic points over the United States and in Europe. But whenever she had a batch of films satisfactory to herself, she was able to unload the responsibility on a committee of ladies and gentleman who represented expert knowledge on as many channels of specialized motion picture exhibition. It was known as the Motion Picture Division of the War Work Council of the Y.M.C.A.[19]

The First World War was crucial to the development of the YMCA as a non-theatrical film distributor. Shortly after America's entry into the conflict, the YMCA, with funding from the American Red Cross, acquired at auction almost the total film library of the bankrupt Lubin Film Manufacturing Company (located in Philadelphia), which was to form the basis of the association's film collection.

In 1917, the Community Motion Picture Bureau took over the Beseler Film Company, which had been founded in June 1915 by Louis R. de Lorme, Henry Major, Jr., and Charles H. Lamb as the Public Educational Film Company. The Community Motion Picture Bureau continued its activities into the 1920s. Its card file and scrapbooks of film reviews culled from contemporary trade papers were eventually acquired by the Library of Congress and formed the basis for much of the original research for the *American Film Institute Catalog: Feature Films 1911–1920*.

If anything, the First World War served as an impetus for the growth of the non-theatrical film. Just as would the Second World War, it illustrated the massive potential for film outside of theatrical presentation. Particularly with the Army Signal Corps, U.S. government film production expanded, and increasingly the federal government and private industry recognized the potential of the motion picture to propagandize, promote, and instruct. Soon after America's entry into the war in Europe, a Committee on Public Information was formed under the chairmanship of George Creel, and in September 1917 it established a Division of Films headed by Charles S. Hart. Creel's study of those years, *How We Advertised the War* (Harper, 1920) by its title alone is indicative of a new mood in the country—promotion and advertising. And what better method of undertaking those two twin tasks than through a relatively new medium, the non-theatrical film.

New companies and new organizations continued to be formed, and often as quickly to disappear, in the 1920s. The term non-theatrical came into common useage at the beginning of the decade. In 1921, Harry

Levey founded National Non-Theatrical Motion Pictures, Inc., which boasted forty-two exchanges, an extensive library of films, and the availability of operators with projectors and screens. "First in the field of industrial film distribution" was its claim. In 1922, a group interested in the non-theatrical use of the motion picture created the Motion Picture Chamber of Commerce. Its purpose was to coordinate the work of various organizations involved in both production and distribution, but it survived only a relatively short period of time and was inactive by 1925.

Interestingly, in that same year Joseph J. Weber published "A Selected and Partially Annotated Bibliography on the Use of Visual Aids in Education."[20] It included the staggeringly high number of sixty-one books and pamphlets.

A familiar name for more than four decades, the Willoughby Movie Library (later known as Willoughby-Peerless) was founded in 1927, when Charles G. Willoughby decided to become involved in 16mm film rentals. In 1929, he advertised that for only $12.50 customers might join the library, "entitling you to your choice of ten reels of star feature films— each reel 400 ft. long—portraying comedies, dramas, cartoons, etc., by Universal and Educational Picture Stars, as well as many others. An average cost of only $1.25 per reel." Charles Willoughby was a pioneer in the retail photographic industry, taking over the Vive Camera Company at 621 Broadway, New York, in 1898 and renaming it Willoughby's. He moved in 1916 to his best-known address on 32nd Street and retired from the business in 1936, when J. G. Dombroff became president.

The 1920s was the decade in which professionals in various fields gave their endorsement to the non-theatrical film. For example, Raymond L. Ditmars of the New York Zoological Society produced in 1925 a series of forty-two reels for use in the teaching of "Living Natural History." In 1930, with the backing of the American Museum of Natural History, Douglas Burden and William Chanler co-produced and directed *The Silent Enemy*, on the lifestyle of the Ojibwa, a North American Indian tribe.[21] The feature-length production was later re-edited as a short subject for school use, but initially it was released theatrically by Paramount and opened at New York's Criterion Theatre on May 19, 1930. "*The Silent Enemy* is interesting, educational and a fine study anywhere, but it has not the commercial draw exhibitors look for," commented *Variety* (May 21, 1930).

While the non-theatrical film is generally associated with short subjects, a surprising number of feature-length films qualify as non-theatrical; from a historical viewpoint, some of the American cinema's first features may well be classified as non-theatrical. The American feature film dates from 1912, and of the eight films released in that year three qualify as non-theatrical: *The Alaska-Siberian Expedition, Atop the World in Motion,* and *Paul J. Rainey's African Hunt.*

The Alaska-Siberian Expedition is a six-reel record of the Carnegie Museum expedition led by Frank E. Kleinschmidt, and when the film first opened in New York in May 1912 it was accompanied with a live lecture by Kleinschmidt (who also photographed the film). *Atop the World in Motion* is discussed elsewhere in this chapter. Paul J. Rainey was a wealthy Cleveland businessman who died on his ranch in Nairobi in 1923. *Paul J. Rainey's African Hunt* is a record of an African safari in which Rainey used packs of dogs to hunt wildlife that he and his fellow hunters could then shoot.

Because the non-theatrical film as such did not exist in 1912, the films just mentioned fall only coincidentally into the non-theatrical genre. The first attempt to produce a non-theatrical feature came in 1923 when Homestead Films, Inc., of Chicago, which had been formed two years earlier, released *The Brown Mouse*, advertised as "A real feature for the Non-Theatrical field." No record of the cast, technical crew, or subject matter of the film has been located.

It was more than twenty years before another attempt was made to produce an entertainment feature exclusively for the non-theatrical market. In 1944, Major 16mm Productions released a Western titled *Sundown Riders*, directed by veteran Lambert Hillyer (who had once worked with William S. Hart) and starring Russell Wade, Jay Kirby, and Andy Clyde. Financed by H. V. George, the feature was shot over an eight-day period in 16mm Kodachrome at a cost of $30,000, considerably less than a black-and-white 35mm Western feature of the same period would have cost to produce.

Sundown Riders was advertised as "the first feature length entertainment picture made by and with professionals and offered for unrestricted exhibition." In its review, *Variety* (October 11, 1944) concentrated on the unique nature of the production: "For years the industry has not only bypassed the rapidly-expanding 16mm field, but has built up resistance to making features available for that branch of the business. A few companies and producers make features available to the miniature field, but only after two or more years [from the original release of the films]. Even the aged subjects have, in many instances, returned surprising grosses from the home, school, and institution circuits."

Feature-length non-theatrical production might be slow in coming and remain virtually experimental throughout the entire history of the genre, but short subject production could only expand in the decades ahead.

NOTES

1. Quoted in Frederick James Smith, "The Evolution of the Motion Picture," *New York Dramatic Mirror*, July 9, 1913, p. 24.
2. Quotes are taken from Rita Horwitz and Harriet Harrison, *The George Kleine*

Collection of Early Motion Pictures in the Library of Congress: A Catalog (Washington, D.C.: Library of Congress, 1980). The Library of Congress holds the films and papers of Kleine.

3. For more information, see Mayfield Bray, *Guide to the Ford Film Collection in the National Archives* (Washington, D.C.: National Archives and Records Service, 1970).

4. John R. Meader, "The Story of the Picture That Moves," *Bohemian Magazine*, September 1908, p. 363.

5. Quoted in Frederick James Smith, "The Evolution of the Motion Picture," *New York Dramatic Mirror*, September 24, 1913, p. 30.

6. Quoted in Smith, "The Evolution of the Motion Picture," p. 25.

7. Nathaniel M. Graham, "Motion Pictures as an Aid to Education," *National Education Association Journal of Proceedings and Addresses*, July 1914, pp. 746–47.

8. See W. R. Rothacker, "C.W. Post Uses Advertising Films," *Motography*, vol. IX, no. 7 (April 1913), p. 222.

9. For more information, see R. E. Doyle, "50 Years of Films," *Business Screen*, vol. XXX, no. 8 (August 1969), p. 32.

10. "Films for Advertising Purposes," in *Minutes* of the Motion Picture Patents Company, October 11, 1910.

11. "Editorials in Films," *New York Dramatic Mirror*, July 1, 1914, p. 21.

12. Arthur Edwin Krows, "Motion Pictures—Not for Theatres," *Educational Screen*, vol. XVII, no. 8 (October 1938), p. 252.

13. Ibid., vol. XVIII, no. 4 (April 1939), p. 124.

14. George Cox, "The Industrial Film—Yesterday and To-Day," *New York Dramatic Mirror*, April 15, 1914, p. 36.

15. Leonard Maltin, *Of Mice and Men* (New York: New American Library, 1980), p. 21.

16. "Jamison Handy—Founder of Business Audiovisuals," *Business Screen*, vol. XXXII, no. 2 (February 1971), p. 33.

17. Ibid., p. 34.

18. Arthur Edwin Krows, "Motion Pictures—Not for Theatres," *Educational Screen*, vol. XIX, no. 2 (February 1940), pp. 60–61.

19. Ibid., vol. XVIII, no. 3 (March 1939), p. 86.

20. Joseph J. Weber, "A Selected and Partially Annotated Bibliography on the Use of Visual Aids in Education," *Educational Screen*, vol. IV, no. 9 (November 1925), pp. 573–76.

21. *The Silent Enemy* is discussed in detail in Kevin Brownlow's *The War, the West, and the Wilderness* (New York: Alfred A. Knopf, 1979).

TWO

Chicago—
The Non-Theatrical Film Capital
of the World

Los Angeles became the center of theatrical filmmaking in the United States for two basic reasons. At a time when filmmaking was still an open-air affair, it offered almost unlimited sunshine. It also was sufficiently far away from New York and the legal machinery of the Motion Picture Patents Company that, through patent controls, sought to monopolize the industry and squash competition by any means, fair or foul.

Just as the choice for the film industry capital of America was between New York and Los Angeles, the competition for the production headquarters of non-theatrical filmmaking was between Chicago and Detroit. The overriding influence on the producers' decision as to where to base their operations was proximity to clients. The Jam Handy Organization relocated from Chicago to Detroit because a major client, General Motors, was there; and so anxious was Handy to impress the client that he even installed a projection room in the General Motors Building so that its executives need not leave the premises in order to approve the latest sponsored production. Wilding Picture Productions had already been established in Detroit for no apparent reason, but according to Arthur Edwin Krows, "Wilding still made the better choice. Chicago was primarily a marketplace. Detroit, on the other hand, commanded the greatest heavy manufacturing section in the country."

Arguing in favor of Detroit, Krows continued,

> Draw a circle of two hundred and fifty miles from Detroit as a center, and
> there are included Chicago, Milwaukee, South Bend, Indianapolis, Day-
> ton, Cincinnati, Pittsburgh, Buffalo, Cleveland, Akron, Toledo and scores
> of other factory points. Increase the spread to four hundred miles, and
> you have Springfield and Louisville—and the national capital, Washing-
> ton, D.C. Another hundred miles, and St. Louis, Nashville, Philadelphia
> and New York swell the roster. However, what is of chief importance lies
> in the first-named ring, including the hearts of the tremendous rubber,
> oil and steel industries. For the greater part a level country, with straight
> roads for automobile caravans, bee-lines for railroads, broad fields every-
> where for airports, and a seaway to Europe through the Great Lakes and
> the St. Lawrence.[1]

Of course much the same argument put forward by Krows for Detroit
could also be offered in favor of Chicago. In the years during which the
non-theatrical industry was growing, Chicago was America's second
city. It was the center for steel production, agricultural machinery, meatpacking, and food processing and second only to New York in clothing
manufacture and printing and publishing. In the years following the
1893 World's Columbian Exposition, Chicago's industrial base became
"among the largest and most diversified in the country."[2] It had one of
the greatest concentrations of heavy industry in the United States, and
the city was considered the most important productive center in the
world. Chicago was the home of America's best-known mail order companies—Sears, Roebuck; Montgomery Ward; and Spiegel—and they
packaged the city's merchandise for shipment all over America.

In its formative years, before the educational film became an important
part of its agenda, the non-theatrical film industry relied on business
and industrial film production. That area of filmmaking could not exist
without sponsors. The corporations, the factories, the business offices
were not in Los Angeles. They were in Chicago, and the non-theatrical
filmmakers went where industry went. Actress Sarah Bernhardt, who
made her first stage appearance in Chicago in 1881, called the city "the
pulse of America."[3] Documenting that pulse was a major aspect of the
non-theatrical film industry.

Further, industrial or business filmmaking was a specialized industry.
Los Angeles had neither the industry nor the need for filmmakers to
specialize. That city was known for theatrical filmmaking, and any production house there was anxious to be a part of that establishment. To
get sidetracked into non-theatrical filmmaking would damage a company's potential for mainstream production.

As important as industry itself were the companies that promoted
business, the advertising agencies. They were the go-betweens for the
non-theatrical producer and the businessman. Few advertising agencies
were directly involved in film production. They relied on non-theatrical

producers, who in turn relied on them. In his 1940 study *American Advertising Agencies: An Inquiry into Their Origin, Growth, Functions and Future*, F. Allen Burt explained:

> An even newer department and one found in only a few agencies is the motion picture, or business film, department. Generally, such work is delegated to professional organizations which specialize in film production, though there are a few agencies which are able to produce films if necessary. An extremely important point in the production of business films is their distribution. An agency may be set up to buy theatre showings, but usually calls in an outside organization to handle any widespread distribution to clubs, churches, schools, and other outlets. This is a job that may require the entire time of a man who can act in the same capacity as the advance agent of a circus or theatrical performance where showings, publicity, ticket distribution, sampling (where feasible), calls on jobbers and dealers, and other missionary work must be done.[4]

American advertising agencies date back to 1840 and have, by tradition, usually been headquartered in New York. As early as 1865, there were two—Charles H. Scriven and Cook, Coburn, and Mack—in Chicago. In 1868, a third agency, Shap and Thain, was founded in Chicago; one of its first clients was Field, Leiter & Company (later renamed Marshall Field & Company). Chicago was never to become the primary locale for American advertising agencies, but it was second only to New York, and there was not a major agency that did not maintain an office in the city.

The Agate, the first advertising club in the world, was founded in Chicago in 1893. In 1912, the American Association of Advertising Agencies was established in the city. Most important of all, it was in Chicago in 1914 that the Audit Bureau of Circulation, which documented the readership of American newspapers and periodicals and thus established their advertising potential, was founded.

Although it might well be argued that the one is dependent upon the other, a final reason for Chicago's continued eminence in non-theatrical film production was the enlightened attitude of the University of Chicago's regents and faculty toward educational films. The university's Dr. George Amos Dorsey, a professor of anthropology, had filmed a series of short subjects on India, China, and Japan, which were released by Universal in 1916. Three years later, Forest Ray Moulton, a professor of astronomy, worked actively with Harley Clarke to establish the Society for Visual Education. In 1922, the Commonwealth Fund made a grant of $10,000 to the university's Frank N. Freeman, enabling him to undertake a study of the use of visual aids in the classroom. Freeman's work was published in 1924 under the title *Visual Education* by the University of Chicago Press. In the 1930s, ERPI Classroom Films prospered because its management had the foresight to seek endorsement from the university, and later the university received acclaim for its acquisition and expansion of the company.

The University of Chicago's presence in the city was instrumental in the creation of the first two major educational film periodicals, *Visual Education* in 1920 and *The Educational Screen* in 1922. The choice of Chicago as publication home for *Business Screen* in 1938 was further evidence of the city's importance to the non-theatrical film. Although headquartered for most of its life in New York, the Educational Film Library Association came about as a result of a meeting held in Chicago, and it was to the Chicago suburbs that the association eventually relocated in 1987.

An important subsidiary publication of *The Educational Screen* was *1000 and One: The Blue Book of Non-Theatrical Films*, first published in 1924. Year after year, this annual published a complete listing of the year's non-theatrical releases, classifying each by category, with a brief description and information as to source. Prior to *The Educational Screen's* publishing *The Blue Book*, earlier editions were published by *Moving Picture Age*.

Chicago was home to two major pioneering production companies, the Selig Polyscope Company, founded in 1896, and the Essanay Film Manufacturing Company, founded in 1907. As early as April and May 1907, Selig made films for Armour and Company, documenting its slaughterhouse and meatpacking plant at the Chicago stockyards. Armour used the footage for public relations purposes in fighting allegations against the meat industry made by Upton Sinclair in his novel *The Jungle*.

Another film from Selig worthy of mention is *The Coming of Columbus*, a three-reel production shot in the fall of 1911 and released in May 1912. Starring Charles Clary in the title role, with Kathlyn Williams as Queen Isabella of Spain, the film was one of the first major productions devoted to American history and found continued exhibition in educational circles as late as 1930. As an educational subject, however, it was something of an oddity for Selig; of the two Chicago producers, it was Essanay (headed by George K. Spoor and G. M. "Bronco Billy" Anderson) that demonstrated more of an interest in the production of educational films.

Selig expired in the early 1920s, by which time it had relocated to Los Angeles, while Essanay ceased production in 1918. In their declining years, both companies became associated for distribution purposes with another Chicago-based concern, the George Kleine Optical Company, founded in Chicago in 1907 and a pioneer in educational film distribution.

Chicago was also home to a third prominent early production house, the Industrial Film Company, founded in December 1909 by Carl Laemmle, Watterson R. Rothacker, and R. H. Cochrane. Laemmle and

Cochrane had entered the film industry in Chicago in 1906, operating a nickelodeon and later a film exchange, the Laemmle Film Service. In 1909, Laemmle established the IMP (Independent Motion Picture) Company, embarking on a film production program that would lead in three years to the formation of Universal. Unlike Selig and Essanay, Laemmle was an independent producer, unattached and antagonistic toward the Motion Picture Patents Company. The creation of the Industrial Film Company at the same time as the establishment of IMP indicates that Laemmle was foresighted enough to realize there was an upcoming need for both industrial and theatrical film production. However, he decided to concentrate his efforts on the latter and in 1913 sold his interest in the Industrial Film Company to Watterson R. Rothacker (1885–1960).

Rothacker has the distinction to be the first, and possibly the only, industrial filmmaker to be the subject of a feature article in the fan magazine *Photoplay*. An unidentified *Photoplay* journalist writing in 1918 described Rothacker as "the first man in America to use film for industrial purposes." The writer continued: "During 1910 and 1911 he did considerable picture missionary work, appearing before various advertising and commercial associations through the country, desiring to interest them in motion picture advertising. He also wrote another series of articles on this subject which appeared in the Scientific American, Printer's Ink, the London Bioscope [a film trade paper], and certain European advertising and selling journals. Such an impression did he make that his new evangelism was translated into every language of Western Europe."[5]

The trade paper the *New York Dramatic Mirror* also endorsed Rothacker's claim as the definitive pioneer in the field, writing in 1914 that his "company has the distinction of being the first company ever organized to specialize in moving pictures adapted for industrial and exploitation, commercial education, and general advertising."[6]

Among the films credited to Rothacker, dates for which are impossible to document, are *Farming with Dynamite*, produced for the Du Pont Powder Company to show farmers how to break up hardpan soil with dynamite, and *The Fixation of Atmospheric Nitrogen*, for the American Cyanamid Company, illustrating the potential of water power for food crop expansion. Other companies for which Rothacker produced films between 1915 and 1920 include H. J. Heinz, Armour (a film on the manufacture of oleomargarine), the Winchester Repeating Arms Company, Western Electric, and Sears, Roebuck. At least two of the films are claimed by *Photoplay* to be feature-length.

In a comment that might well be an endorsement of advertising on television today, Rothacker said, "The best advertisement in the world will never be written, because moving pictures are the superlative advertising medium and exceed the limitations of any pen."[7]

In 1916, the name of the Industrial Film Company was changed to the Rothacker Film Manufacturing Company. By that time Rothacker had also established a film laboratory, which handled developing and printing for the Essanay Company and claimed to print and develop more film than any other laboratory in the United States. "I built my laboratory in Chicago," said Rothacker, "because it is my firm belief that Chicago will eventually be the place where all film manufacturing will be done, situated as it is, so centrally."[8]

In later years, it was the laboratory rather than the production house that brought in the greater profit. It handled developing and printing for many of Chicago's non-theatrical filmmakers and, additionally, gained a reputation for specialized work. The optical effects for the 1925 science fiction classic *The Lost World* were created by Rothacker.

In 1926, the company was reorganized and given the more modern-sounding name of Rothacker Industrial Films. That same year it was acquired by Herbert J. Yates, best remembered in later years as the head of Republic Pictures. Rothacker continued in the film industry, working for First National, ERPI, Paramount, and the Quigley Publishing Company (publisher of *Motion Picture Herald* and *Motion Picture Almanac*). During the Second World War, he served as chairman of the Los Angeles Board of Review of Motion Pictures for the Office of Censorship. Rothacker died in Santa Monica, California, on January 25, 1960, at the age of seventy-five.

The one Chicago company that grew with the non-theatrical film industry and that by its presence in the city encouraged others to locate there was Bell & Howell. Incorporated on February 20, 1907, the company was formed by a projectionist named Donald J. Bell (b.1896) and an engineer/inventor named Albert Summers Howell (1879–1951) to manufacture 35mm equipment for the theatrical industry, beginning with a camera and shortly thereafter a printer. The Bell & Howell Co. first became involved in the non-theatrical field in 1919 with the manufacture of 17.5mm equipment for the amateur movie enthusiast. Bell & Howell's major move away from the theatrical field came in 1922, when it began work on perfecting a 16mm camera and projector (introduced the following year).

Dubbing its first projector the Filmo, Bell & Howell established the Show-at-Home Movie Library, Inc., to distribute 16mm films to users of the projector. Short reels, 100 feet in length, consisting of science subjects, cut-down versions of entertainment features, and truncated cartoon shorts, were sold directly to dealers with the suggestion that they establish their own local rental libraries. In 1930 the library announced a major addition of 120 German films produced by the Ufa Company, available in silent or sound-on-disc versions. In the late summer of 1934, Bell & Howell introduced its sound-on-film 16mm rental library, Filmosound, named after the 16mm projector it had introduced the previous year, with H. A. Spanuth, who had built up the company's silent film library, heading the new concern.

In 1935, when Spanuth joined Ideal, William F. Kruse became the library's general manager. Although Spanuth took many of the Bell & Howell titles with him to Ideal, the Filmosound Library was able to add many new titles as a result of a deal with Gaumont-British whereby the English concern marketed Bell & Howell projectors in Europe under its name in return for making 16mm prints of its releases available to the American market.

In 1945, the Bell & Howell Co. became a public company and dropped the definite article from its name. The following year, the Filmosound Library was sold to Universal Pictures. On July 24, 1946, the company entered the microfilm industry with the purchase of the microfilm division of Pathe Manufacturing Company. The sale of Filmosound was far from indicative of the demise of Bell & Howell's non-theatrical activities. In June 1954 it purchased the assets of the DeVry Corporation and in July 1967 acquired Wilding Picture Productions (subsequently sold in 1980 to Maritz, Inc., of St. Louis).

Bell & Howell Co., which for more than seventy years had been a legendary name in both the theatrical and non-theatrical fields, severed all its connections with the film industry in 1983, disposing of its instrumentation line of business and concentrating on business records management and microfilm publishing through its subsidiary Universal Microfilms.

Major production houses active in Chicago in the 1920s include Homestead Films, Inc.; the Kinema Film Service; Super Photoplay Service; the Society for Visual Education, Inc.; Picture Service Corporation; and the Atlas Educational Film Company. The last was founded in 1913 by two brothers, I. R. and C. A. Rehm. A third brother, R. R. Rehm, and a brother-in-law, T. L. Haines, founded a sister company of the same name in San Francisco. The Advance Motion Picture Company was founded in Chicago in 1912. Filmack Studios was established there also, by Irving Mack, and remains active through the present, primarily in the production of television commercials.

Burton Holmes (1870–1958) was born in Chicago and established Burton Holmes Films, Inc., in the city as an outgrowth of his lecture activities. Aside from production, Holmes operated his own film laboratory, initially headed by Oscar Depue, who had been with Holmes as early as 1896.

In the 1930s, some twenty-five major non-theatrical companies were headquartered in Chicago. As late as 1972, when the market was about to take a downward plunge, Chicago had thirty-five active non-theatrical production companies, among the more prominent of which were Cavalcade Productions, Inc. (founded 1948); Academy Film Productions, Inc. (founded 1950); Telecine Film Studios, Inc. (founded 1952); and Henry Ushijima Films, Inc. (founded 1962).

As well as production, Chicago was equally prominent as the manufacturing and distribution center for non-theatrical equipment. Aside from the Bell & Howell Co., Chicago was home to lesser companies, including Fitzpatrick & McElroy, the American Projectoscope Co., the Holmes Projector Company, the Bass Camera Company, the American Projecting Company, the Acme Motion Picture Projector Company, and the Movie Supply Co. Arguably as important as the Bell & Howell Co. in the manufacture of projection equipment was the DeVry Corp., which had two incarnations.

Herman A. DeVry (1876–1941) immigrated to the United States from his native Germany and came to Chicago in 1911, working first as a cameraman for Rothacker. In 1914, he founded the DeVry Corp. in the city, introducing a portable 35mm projector that could be carried in its own suitcase, which helped to spread the use of industrial films by traveling salesmen. The original DeVry Corp. was acquired by the Q.R.S. Player Piano Roll Co. in 1929, and Herman DeVry left the company in 1931. That same year he founded the new DeVry Corp. under the initial name of Herman A. DeVry, Inc.

In the 16mm field, DeVry introduced its first sound-on-film projector in 1934. It was a worthy competitor to the RCA sound-on-film projector, first marketed in 1932, and the Bell & Howell Filmosound projector introduced the following year. The advantage that both Bell & Howell and RCA had over DeVry was that both operated major film libraries as support operations for owners of their projectors. Bell & Howell's film library dated back to the 1920s, while in February 1933 RCA Victor announced the creation of a 16mm sound-on-film library, with 400-foot reels on a variety of educational subjects.

The advantage that DeVry as an individual had over RCA and Bell & Howell was that he was an ardent and well-liked supporter of film as an educational tool. As early as 1925, he founded the Summer School of Visual Education, which later became the National Conference on Visual Education. In 1940, he produced a series of forty educational sound subjects under the general title of "Filmsets in World Geography."

In March 1945, DeVry announced that it would expand its distribution and equipment operations, but it sold off its laboratory equipment to Filmack Studios. By the following year, DeVry boasted a 16mm rental library consisting of 400 feature films, 28 serials, 58 musical Westerns, and 64 Westerns. The bulk of the titles were from RKO and Universal; the latter was the mainstay of many 16mm rental libraries, with, for example, Bell & Howell in direct competition with DeVry in the same city making available more than one hundred of the studio's releases. In 1954, DeVry's remaining assets were acquired by Bell & Howell.

A third major equipment manufacturer in Chicago, but of relatively little importance in the non-theatrical field, was Ampro Corporation, founded in 1929 by Axel Monson. The latter retired from the company three years after its 1944 acquisition by General Precision Equipment.

Aside from non-theatrical producers and equipment manufacturers, Chicago was home to two major 16mm rental libraries, Ideal and Films Inc. In addition, many smaller rental libraries made their home there, as well as 16mm film rental branches of the National Film Board of Canada and the British Information Services.

Ideal Pictures Corporation was acclaimed in the 1940s as the largest 16mm film rental library in the world, with offices in New York, Los Angeles, Miami, New Orleans, Memphis, Dallas, Denver, Atlanta, Portland, Oregon, and Richmond, Virginia. Its founder Bertram Willoughby (1881–1948) was a Canadian who became interested in the use of films while a Congregational minister in the American midwest. He began to produce a series of animated "Sermonettes" prior to the First World War. He was named vice president and religious director of New Era Films, but that company was destroyed by fire in 1918; the following year Willoughby formed the Pilgrim Photoplay Exchange in Chicago as a 35mm rental library for religious subjects.

At some point in the 1920s, the company name was changed to Ideal. It expanded beyond the religious film market and embraced 16mm when it came into general use in the mid-1920s. In 1941, Willoughby formed Bertram Willoughby Pictures, Inc., in New York as an affiliate company, and it absorbed Arrow Film Service. The year after Willoughby's death, a majority interest in Ideal was acquired by Coronet/Esquire, Inc.

Active through the 1960s, Ideal handled the exclusive 16mm release of films from RKO and Allied Artists and also handled some titles from United Artists, PRC, Warner Bros., and Walt Disney Productions. It appears to have specialized in black entertainment films, presumably intended primarily for black American 16mm audiences, listing forty "All-Negro Cast Features" in its 1950 catalog, but only thirty-three titles in 1959. Ideal handled a considerable number of 16mm silent films, but it appears to have sold off the bulk of those titles in 1950 to Willoughby-Peerless.[9]

Ideal's position as America's leading 16mm distributor of entertainment films was taken over in the 1960s by Films Incorporated, which made its corporate headquarters in the Chicago suburb of Wilmette.

Films Incorporated (or Films Inc., as it is more generally known) was founded by one of the pioneers in 16mm film distribution, Orton W. Hicks (b.1900), a graduate of Dartmouth College who beginning in 1958 was to serve as its vice president. Upon leaving Dartmouth, Hicks joined the training program for college graduates at Eastman Kodak on May 15, 1922. He worked at Eastman Kodak's retail stores in Boston and New York until 1926, when he became vice president of the Gillette Camera Stores. As he recalled in 1948:

> Running a camera store myself, I became aware of opportunities to supply needs which weren't being met by the Kodascope Libraries at the time, so I got together a group of about 20 dealers from various parts of the country to subscribe to the company I formed called "Home Film Libraries, Inc." It was a home film library, all right—I ran it at home, nights. But by December 1929, two years later, it had grown sufficiently to justify my leaving Gillette and devoting my full time to it.
>
> A natural by-product of this library was supplying entertainment films and equipment to steamships. The big ships already at that time had 35mm equipment, orchestras, everything. So I went to see the smaller ships, found they couldn't see investing large money in equipment. That was in the early 1930s—depression—and good 16mm projectors were available through pawnshops at $25 apiece. So I went around locating and buying them, and loaned them to steamships so long as they would rent their pictures from me.[10]

In December 1935, the name of the company was changed to Films Inc. In an effort to provide major entertainment features to 16mm users, Hicks had signed a contract with Paramount in August 1935, making it the first Hollywood studio to release its sound films in 16mm. To emphasize the change in policy, Films Inc., ran an advertisement in the January 1936 issue of *The Educational Screen* announcing, "At last! Rent First Run Productions in 16mm Sound-on-Film." In reality the listed titles were all British productions, such as *Evergreen, Chu Chin Chow,* and *The Iron Duke.* The Paramount titles did not become available in bulk until the summer of 1938, when Films Inc., announced the release of seventy-five features, study guides for many of which had been prepared by Recreational and Educational Guides, Inc.

Orton W. Hicks left Films Inc., in August 1938 to become chairman of the board of the Walter O. Gutlohn Corporation, which he has identified as the first independent *national* 16mm rental library. The corporation was founded in 1933 by a doctor named Walter O. Gutlohn and an attorney, Harry A. Kapit. Gutlohn died in 1937, and the corporation continued under the management of Kapit and Gutlohn's widow Blanche.

Gutlohn pioneered the distribution of 16mm sound subjects, initially on disc and then on film, with its first release being a three-reel comedy short titled *Pusher in the Face,* starring Raymond Griffith. Hicks recalled:

The Gutlohn organization also pioneered deposit libraries at universities, with Indiana the first of these; and it was the first library to arrange for deferred payments so little people around the country could get into the library business. The company had great faith in the little fellow. Some of them got quite big. First of the big ones Gutlohn Library helped start in sound was Bert Willoughby of Ideal Pictures. Gutlohn also had the first film libraries in CCC camps—Harry Kapit made the deal for the 100 or so in the 4th Corps Area of the U.S. Army. I think this was the first time any film library had a contract for government service, both educational and entertainment.[11]

Hicks remained with Gutlohn until 1945, when the corporation was sold to George A. Hirliman's International Theatrical and Television Corporation. The latter also acquired Certified Film Distributors, which acted as the sales organization for Gutlohn, making its films available to photographic dealers, department stores, and the like. At the time of the sale it was reported that Gutlohn was grossing more than one million dollars a year and maintained a library of more than 3,000 subjects. Two years later, Gutlohn's assets were purchased by New York–based Library Films, Inc.

While not, of course, a suburb of Chicago—it is the fourth largest city in Iowa—Davenport is close enough to that metropolis to be linked with it; and the establishment and development there of two companies that played a large part in the history of the non-theatrical film are in many ways directly related to the proximity of the two cities. Blackhawk Films will be discussed elsewhere; pre-eminent in the growth of 8mm and 16mm for home use, it was located in Davenport for its entire active life, as was the Victor Animatograph Company, the fourth major projector and camera manufacturer to be located in the Chicago area and one almost as important in its day as Bell & Howell.

The Victor Animatograph Company was founded and operated for almost its entire existence by Alexander F. (Ferdinand) Victor (1878–1961). Born in Sweden, he claimed to have been exhibiting the Lumière films as early as 1896. Victor came to the United States as a magician on the vaudeville stage in 1900 and was billed as "The Great Alexander," a billing which *Film News* suggested should remain with him as a pioneer in the 16mm film field.

On April 1, 1910, Victor established the Victor Animato–Graph [sic] Company in Davenport, Iowa, with capitalization from ten of the city's business leaders. Here he developed a film and projecting machine for home use, which the *Davenport Daily Times* (June 17, 1910) reported, "promises to revolutionize the motion picture business . . . as it will enable any person to take the motion pictures, develop and print them, and reproduce them on a screen in a simple manner and at small cost.

It gives promise of making the motion picture machine as common and as popular in the home as the graphophone [i.e., the phonograph]."

Victor's overwhelming interest was in developing film equipment for non-theatrical use. In March 1914, he introduced a 35mm home movie outfit, the Animatograph. From 1911 onward, he developed and marketed glass slide stereo viewers and projectors. Considering 28mm as the logical, and at that time only, film gauge for non-theatrical use, primarily because it was acetate-based rather than nitrate-based film and therefore non-flammable, Victor invented a 28mm reduction printer during the First World War. He persuaded two Chicago production houses that were nearing the end of their lives, George Kleine and Essanay, to agree to his reducing their films to 28mm; and in 1919 he announced the creation of the 28mm-based Victor Home Cinema.

Such a staunch supporter was Victor of substandard film for non-theatrical use that in 1918 he appeared before the Society of Motion Picture Engineers, meeting in Rochester, New York, and argued for a new and separate standard for motion pictures outside the theatrical arena, suggesting a modification of Pathé's 28mm. As a result of Victor's urging, the standard of 1.102 inches (28mm) was adopted for safety standard film, for use with portable projectors, in April 1918.

Despite his earlier advocacy of 28mm film, Victor was far from slow in adopting 16mm film stock when it was introduced by Eastman Kodak; indeed, his company was one of the first to provide equipment for use with the new gauge. In August 1923, 16mm cameras and projectors were introduced by the Victor Animatograph Company; the first sound-on-disc 16mm projector was marketed in 1930; and three years later Victor introduced a 16mm sound-on-film projector, the Animatophone. By the late 1940s, Victor had three 16mm sound projectors available—the Victor Envoy, the Victor Lite-Weight, and the Victor Triumph 60—as well as three 16mm cameras—the Victor Models 3, 4, and 5—with the last being "an ultra-refined camera with reverse action for those whose specialty is trick photography."

There is no question that the Victor Animatograph Company was innovative, and yet competition was such in the 1930s that the company suffered a severe financial slump, from which it recovered only as a result of the increased demand for 16mm equipment during the Second World War. In June 1946, the company was acquired by the Curtiss-Wright Corporation, which expanded its operations into the manufacture of 35mm slide and filmstrip projectors. Financial losses forced yet another sale of the company in December 1950, to the Bendix Corporation, with Victor's projector line of products being purchased by the Whittemore-Eastern Corporation. On May 1, 1951, a group of employees bought out the company, renaming it the Victor Animatograph Corporation of Iowa. Five years later, a final takeover by the Kalart Corporation ended Victor's forty-six years of existence in Davenport, Iowa.

Writing of Alexander Victor in the *Journal of the Society of Motion Picture and Television Engineers*, Samuel G. Rose commented:

> When nearly 80, Victor summarized his early life by saying that he had been an "exhibitor, cameraman, producer, studio owner, script writer and twice an actor." He could have added inventor, designer and manufacturer. Victor had an insatiable enthusiasm and prophetic vision for designing and building equipment to meet the needs of the time in the rapidly changing field of nontheatrical equipment. . . . His interest and enthusiasm never waned and he met "head-on" each new challenge presented to him by designing and producing apparatus to satisfy the needs of the amateur, of industry, of education and of government. . . . Alexander Victor played an important part in the birth and growth of the nontheatrical motion-picture industry.[12]

Each year, the theatrical industry's trade annual *Motion Picture Almanac* publishes a listing of "producers, distributors, or libraries of nontheatrical motion pictures." The number of entries through the years has dwindled considerably, and by 1991 there were only sixty-seven entries. Not surprisingly, the largest number, seventeen, are located in New York. Los Angeles and environs comes third with five. But Chicago is still there, holding second place with seven active companies.

NOTES

1. Arthur Edwin Krows, "Motion Pictures—Not for Theatres," *Educational Screen*, vol. XIX, no. 2 (February 1940), p. 58.

2. Harold M. Mayer and Richard C. Wade, *Chicago: Growth of a Metropolis* (Chicago: University of Chicago Press, 1969).

3. Quoted on the title page of Edward Wagenknecht, *Chicago* (Norman: University of Oklahoma Press, 1964).

4. F. Allen Burt, *American Advertising Agencies: An Inquiry into Their Origins, Growth, Functions and Future* (New York: Harper & Brothers, 1940), p. 25.

5. "A Specialist in a Fine Art," *Photoplay*, vol. XV, no. 1 (December 1918), p. 57.

6. *New York Dramatic Mirror*, May 20, 1914, p. 28.

7. "A Specialist in a Fine Art," *Photoplay*, vol. XV, no. 1 (December 1918), p. 58.

8. Ibid.

9. According to Hal Guthrie in a letter to the author, June 10, 1985.

10. "Orton Hicks Reminisces," *Film News*, vol. VIII, no. 12 (June–July 1948), p. 10.

11. Ibid.

12. Samuel G. Rose, "Alexander F. Victor—Motion Picture Pioneer," *Journal of the SMPTE*, vol. LXXII, no. 8 (August 1963), p. 621.

THREE

The Eastman Kodak Connection

To the layman, the best-known pioneer in the evolution of the American film industry is Thomas Alva Edison. Yet his supposed position as the father of the motion picture can easily be challenged, not by his relatively unknown associate W.K.L. Dickson (who is deserving of the credit for most of Edison's inventions in this field), but by George Eastman (1854–1932), whose introduction of transparent roll film in 1889 made practical motion picture photography a reality. The film was a strip of clear cellulose nitrate, two-and-a-half inches or 70mm wide, coated with black-and-white photographic emulsion; Edison split the film in two for use in his camera and projector, creating the theatrical film standard gauge of 35mm, although it was not completely recognized as such until 1903. In 1892, George Eastman renamed his company Eastman Kodak, and it remains to the present the most famous name in the history of motion picture and still photography. George Eastman is one of a handful of American industrialists whose names have become household words, perhaps the only one whose name has symbolized quality and reliability for more than one hundred years.

In 1888, George Eastman introduced his first Kodak roll film camera, choosing a trade name that could be spelled and pronounced simply in any language and that began and ended with his favorite letter, K. Along with the camera, Eastman introduced a slogan which has continued in popular usage down the years, "You press the button—we do the rest."

Having introduced a still camera for home and non-professional use, it is not surprising that Eastman Kodak should have worked on the development of a movie camera for the same market. The result was the Cine Kodak 16mm camera, introduced in January 1923 and formally presented and discussed at the May 1923 meeting of the Society of Motion Picture Engineers in Atlantic City.

J. G. Capstaff of the Eastman Kodak Research Laboratories had been developing the project for a number of years, and in 1920 he asked the Hawk-Eye camera company to build a prototype 16mm hand-cranked camera. In 1921, Capstaff shot a number of 16mm test films to show to George Eastman. To illustrate the potential of the new gauge for home movie use, Capstaff filmed *A Child's Birthday Party*, a record of the tenth birthday celebration of Charles Gleason, whose father played the organ at receptions hosted by George Eastman. Although forgotten and not screened in recent memory, *A Child's Birthday Party* is every bit as important in 16mm film history as is the Lumière Brothers 1895 film *Le Repas de Bébé* in the development of theatrical filmmaking.

The industrial and educational use of 16mm was also acknowledged by Capstaff in 1921, when he photographed the activities of the Research Laboratory under the title *Some Chemical Reactions*. That same year, Capstaff's associate Harris Tuttle filmed what are obviously the first medical films in 16mm, the record of a child suffering from Oppenheim's disease and the delivery of a baby by cesarean section. The following year, Tuttle filmed the manufacture of fireproof bricks and cement blocks, as well as a slow-motion study of workers at Kodak Park, intended to record how one worker could outperform another by as much as 25 percent.

George Eastman succumbed to the lure of 16mm in 1926, when he took a home movie camera with him on a photo safari to Africa, with his friends Osa and Martin Johnson and Carl Akeley.

Eastman Kodak pioneered further developments in the 16mm field in the 1920s, including negative film (the original film was reversal only), color, and sound. Experiments in 8mm film began in 1928 at the Kodak Research Laboratories, and the first cameras and projectors for that gauge were marketed by Eastman Kodak in August 1932.

Aside from marketing its own 16mm film equipment, Eastman Kodak agreed to process not only all film shot in its cameras but also film shot on rival equipment. It was an important decision not only in the promotion of 16mm but also as evidence of the company's willingness to work with everyone in the field. In many respects it might have been practical to follow the French Pathé Company and market a substandard, non-theatrical film gauge of 17.5mm, which is, of course, 35mm film split in two. Eastman Kodak rejected 17.5mm in part because of that fact. If it were nothing more than 35mm halved, the film available to non-theatrical and home users might well be nitrate-based, highly inflammable and dangerous. To avoid such a problem, the company adopted 16mm; and after discussions with representatives from Victor and Bell & Howell determined that 16mm films should be made only on acetate, or safety base, stock. Through 1950, 35mm nitrate films continued in use in the United States, but since the introduction of 16mm in 1923, there has never been a 16mm nitrate film.

If it had accomplished nothing more than the introduction of 16mm film, Eastman Kodak would deserve a prominent place in the history of the non-theatrical genre. After all, without 16mm, the industry could not have expanded as rapidly into the home, office, and classroom. In that the cost of purchase and processing of 16mm film stock was estimated to be one-sixth that of 35mm, the Eastman Kodak invention made non-theatrical filmmaking an economically viable proposition. Without 16mm, the coming of sound could well have heralded the demise of much non-theatrical filmmaking.

Yet Eastman Kodak did far more in the field than merely introduce 16mm and 8mm. It created two major subsidiaries to service the new medium, the Kodascope Libraries for the 16mm and 8mm home user and Eastman Teaching Films for classroom use.

The Kodascope Libraries were founded by Willard Beach Cook (1871–1952), who is often cited as the "Father of the Non-Theatrical Film." Born in Erie, Pennsylvania, and the youngest graduate in civil engineering from the University of Virginia, Cook was involved in structural-steel engineering in both Chicago and New York. In 1912, he saw a demonstration in London of the Pathéscope 28mm film projector. That year, 28mm had been introduced by the French Pathé Company in a determined effort to replace 17.5mm, which had been in existence as a substandard film gauge since 1898. Portable and mounted on a wooden base, the projector, called the "Kok" in a phonetic rendering of "Coq," the Pathé cockerel trade-mark, resembled a Singer sewing machine.

Cook acquired the U.S. rights to the machinery and in 1913 established the Pathescope Company of America, marketing the 28mm projector as the Premier Pathescope. Early financial backing for the new company came from vaudeville entrepreneur Percy G. Williams and from John T. Underwood of the Underwood typewriter family. Initially, Cook purchased the 28mm films directly from Pathé Freres in Paris, but in 1916 he founded his own laboratory in Long Island City, where 35mm films were reduced to 28mm. The raw stock also was first shipped from France, but later Eastman Kodak began to make it available. It was claimed to be non-flammable, but tests in recent years indicate that it does contain some nitrate film stock and that 28mm is subject to the same decomposition process as 35mm nitrate film.

"The going was difficult at first," remembered Cook, "as we were alone in the 28mm field until Mr. [Alexander] Victor came along and began also to make 28mm, the Victor Home Cinema. Far from resenting his competition, we welcomed it, and benefited by it because, before that time, we were constantly hearing the argument: 'What if you go out of business?' "[1] By 1919, Pathescope offered a choice of 1,500 films in its library of features and short subjects, entertainment and educational in content.

In its early years, the organization marketed a 28mm projector and camera for around $400, a price based on Cook's premise that his equipment was not for the masses but for the top 400. However, by marketing a camera Cook was demonstrating that 28mm could be used not only to photograph family and friends but also to make in-house business films. Following the First World War, Pathescope actively embarked on industrial film production, with Clinton F. Ives heading the division until 1938 (by which time, of course, Pathescope had long abandoned the 28mm field; its laboratory started 16mm reduction printing in 1923).

(One of Pathescope's industrial division salesmen, Edward A. Stevenson, was appointed president of another industrial film company, Visugraphic Pictures, Inc., in 1924. Founded in 1921, Visugraphic was a leading New York non-theatrical film producer of the 1920s. In 1929 Stevenson wrote a promotional book for the company titled *Motion Pictures for Advertising and Selling*. Visugraphic did not survive the sound revolution and entered bankruptcy in 1933.)

Willard Beach Cook developed a friendship with Dr. C.E.L. Mees, director of the Eastman Kodak Research Laboratories, from the time the company agreed to provide 28mm film stock. When Eastman Kodak decided to organize the Kodascope Libraries to provide 16mm prints for home use, Mees recommended Cook to George Eastman as the ideal organizer of the division. Cook continued to operate the Pathescope Company of America and installed the new Kodascope Libraries, Inc., in an adjoining office at New York's Aeolian Building.

The Kodascope Libraries, Inc., were formed in 1923 but did not become operational until 1925, offering 16mm prints for rental only from various regional offices and from local camera stores. To join the Kodascope Libraries, customers were required to pay a fee of $25—the figure remained the same in the 1920s and 1930s—which was refundable when the borrower decided to discontinue service. The first catalog of the Kodascope Libraries was published in 1925, followed by new editions in 1926, 1928, 1930, 1932, 1936, and the late 1930s. Borrowers were encouraged to loan films for one night only and return them promptly, with the company explaining, "A Film library is like a Book library in that it is subject to constantly changing demands for the subjects in its possession. Unlike a Public Library, however, a Film library is a business institution, which must earn its expense and a fair return upon the capital invested, and it is quite evident that this can be done only by keeping the films continually in use."

Eastman Kodak encouraged photographic supplies and equipment dealers to become regional branches of the Kodascope Libraries, explaining in an advertisement of the period, "The Kodascope Libraries' Dealer-Distributor Franchise (1) insures maximum profit without speculative risk to the Dealer, and (2) furnishes greatest satisfaction to the Customer through a constant supply of fresh subjects from the world's greatest producers, exchangeable every four months. Every Distributor has also available on a commission basis the entire Kodascope repertoire from our nearest Branch Library."

The Kodascope Libraries were organized in much the same manner as Cook's Pathescope library, with the same variety of subjects, all of which were given numbers based on their type: Travel, Sports, Manners, and Customs were numbered from 1,000 up; Industries and Agriculture from 2,000; Popular Science, Useful Arts, and Natural History from 3,000; Comedies and Juvenile items from 4,000; Religious subjects from 5,000; Reconstructed and Modern History films from 6,000; Animated Cartoon Comedies from 7,000; and Dramas from 8,000.

Catalogs, priced at ten cents each, numbered more than one hundred pages and by the 1930s were available in three categories: 16mm Silent, 8mm Silent, and 16mm Sound. Of course, the Kodascope Libraries were exclusively 16mm until 1932, when an 8mm library was introduced. More than 700 titles were ultimately listed in the catalogs, with short subjects usually released in their entirety and features edited down to five reels.

Eastman Kodak acquired its first major group of feature-length productions for the libraries from Warner Bros. An agreement dated May 27, 1926, had the Kodascope Libraries "given rights forever and without restrictions on the 16mm pictures *The Clash of the Wolves, The Lighthouse by the Sea, Lady Windermere's Fan, His Majesty, Bunker Bean* and *The Man on the Box*."[2] Additional Warner Bros. titles were added later, as well as eight Larry Semon short comedies, produced by Vitagraph (later acquired by Warner Bros.). On June 15, 1927, the Kodascope Libraries contracted for a first group of Paramount features.

Interestingly, the rights acquired by Eastman Kodak were not limited to 16mm, but the company had permission to make "miniature reproductions not exceeding 28 millimeters in width for non-theatrical exhibition."[3] The license fees paid by Eastman Kodak were relatively small; Warner Bros. asked for $1,000 for each of its feature films, while the license fees for the Paramount releases varied according to the popularity of the film. The Western epic *The Covered Wagon* (1923) was licensed to Eastman Kodak for $2,000, but the feature *Behind the Front* (1926) cost the company $5,000. According to film historian David Pierce, who has made an extensive study of the Kodascope Libraries, these fees were high compared to the amounts paid by Eastman Kodak when first establishing the libraries in 1924. It paid George Kleine a mere $75 per title for two educational subjects, *Caring for Birds in Winter* and *Getting Acquainted with Bees*.

Pierce writes, "The titles were handled by Kodascope library exchanges, which were established initially in six U.S. cities and Toronto. By 1930 the catalogs were boasting about 15 US, four Canadian, and 21 overseas locations for the rental and sale of films. Not all titles were available to each Kodascope exchange. For example, Minneapolis had the half of the library with odd control numbers, while Kansas City had only the even numbered subjects. Of course, camera stores licensed only the titles they wanted."[4] As of 1931, there were fifty-one dealer-distributors.

Films in the Kodascope Libraries were for rental, not sale; but increasingly members were asking Eastman Kodak to make titles available for sale. In answer to such requests, in May 1927 the company introduced Kodak Cinegraph 16mm films (called Ciné Kodagraphs in the United Kingdom) available for both rental and sale. In the same category, Cinegraph Eight Films were introduced in 1932. Prices for the 8mm titles were relatively low and remained stable throughout the 1930s: $2.00 for a 50 ft. subject; $4.00 for a 100 ft. subject; and $8.00 for a 200 ft. subject. In the 1930s, 16mm prices actually decreased. When first introduced, a 100 ft. film cost $7.50 and a 400 ft. subject was $30.00. By 1931, the prices were $6.00 and $24.00 respectively, and a year later (and for the rest of the decade), a 100 ft. subject cost $5.00 and a 400 ft. reel was $20.00.

In 1939, the Kodascope Libraries, Inc., became a division of Eastman Kodak stores. The ten Universal features and fifteen Universal short subjects in the libraries (including the major studio productions of *My Man Godfrey* and *Show Boat*) were transferred to the Bell & Howell Filmosound Library, which was already handling twenty-seven features, three serials, and fifty-five short subjects from Universal. In 1945, Kodascope Libraries discontinued its operations entirely.

After the demise of the Kodascope Libraries, many collectors were successful in acquiring prints. In that the 16mm films were often reduced directly from 35mm negatives, as well as being tinted and toned, they were often the best possible prints available on a specific title and were much sought after by film collectors. Although a number of the films were protected by copyright, public screenings were arranged by the new owners, a turn of events that caused great consternation at Warner Bros. in 1950. So disturbed was the company by these relatively unimportant public presentations of films it had produced more than twenty years earlier, which had no commercial value whatsoever, that Warner Bros. was able to obtain an assignment back from Eastman Kodak of all the titles which it had originally licensed.

Of course, Warner Bros. was only one of the producers represented in the Kodascope Libraries. Others were Mutual, Paramount, Universal,

Bray, Hal Roach, Mack Sennett, Fox, Truart, Chester, Vitagraph, Cecil B. DeMille, Selznick, F.B.O., Christie, W. W. Hodkinson, Joe Rock, Selig, and Pathé. There was also a sampling of titles from another Eastman Kodak division, Eastman Teaching Films.

George Eastman was one of the most philanthropic of American industrialists in the early years of the twentieth century. In the September 1923 issue of *Hearst's International Magazine*, he commented, "If a man has wealth, he has to make a choice, because there is the money heaping up. He can keep it together in a bunch and then leave it for others to administer after he is dead. Or, he can get it into action and have fun, while he is still alive. I prefer getting it into action and adapting it to human needs, and making the plan work."[5]

Eastman's main concern was with education. He made his first charitable contribution, of $50, to the Massachusetts Institute of Technology in 1887. In 1912, he made an anonymous donation of $1.5 million of Eastman Kodak stock to that same educational institution. During 1924, Eastman made contributions totaling $8.5 million to the University of Rochester, founding both the Rochester Symphony Orchestra and the Eastman School of Music. Biographer Carl W. Ackerman wrote, "In December 1924, he 'signed away' . . . the princely portion of his wealth, dividing it between the University of Rochester, the Massachusetts Institute of Technology, and Hampton and Tuskegee Normal and Agricultural Institutes."[6]

The industrialist had one other major contribution to make to the educational community. It did not involve any great sum of money, but it did benefit from the Eastman Kodak name and reputation. With the introduction of 16mm film in 1923, officials at Eastman Kodak had considered the use of the new gauge in educational filmmaking. From early studies, the company had concluded that films did have educational value, that a major influx of capital was needed for entry into the field, and that projection equipment and the films themselves were too expensive for most schools to acquire.

In March 1926, George Eastman hosted a meeting of educators at his Rochester office. Present were Thomas E. Finnegan, chairman of the Visual Education Committee of the National Education Association; John H. Finley of the *New York Times*; Payson Smith, Massachusetts Commissioner of Education; Mary Pennell of Columbia University; Otis Caldwell, principal of the Lincoln School of Teachers College; William A. McAndrew, Chicago's Superintendent of Schools; Howard Burge, principal of the Fredonia, New York, State Normal School; Herbert S. West, Rochester's Superintendent of Schools; Charles F. Finch, Rochester's Director of Vocational Schools; and Mabel Simpson, Rochester's Primary Grades Supervisor.

As a result of that meeting, Eastman wrote a letter, for publication, to Will H. Hays, president of the Motion Picture Producers and Distributors of America:

> For the last three years the Eastman Kodak Company has been making a survey of the use of motion pictures in teaching as a supplement to textbooks to find out what promise there was of future sound development. Such films were not practicable until an easily operated projector and economical films were available to schools.
>
> The survey led us to the conclusion that very little had been accomplished in producing teaching films suitable for classroom use and that there was little prospect of any organization with the necessary resources attempting to solve the problem. Therefore, after full consideration, the company has decided to approach the solution of this problem in an experimental way.
>
> It proposes to make a number of teaching films closely correlated with selected courses and in accordance with a definite educational plan. These films will be prepared with the advice and assistance of competent educators and will be put into a limited number of representative schools in different cities for trial in their classrooms. As the work of production goes on, the company will thus have definitive information as to whether the right sort of films are being made.
>
> In making this announcement the company wants it to be clearly understood that it will have no apparatus or films for sale to schools during this experimental period, which will take about two years. Any future developments will be determined by the success of these experiments. The company leaves itself free to discontinue this undertaking at any time it feels that there are insurmountable obstacles to its success.[7]

George Eastman wrote to Will H. Hays because, as early as April 1923, he had urged the National Education Association to sponsor the production of educational films. Further, the Eastman Kodak Company, a member of the Motion Picture Producers and Distributors of America, was anxious to assure its fellow members, to whom it provided raw stock, that the company was not about to embark on an active production program in direct competition with the theatrical film industry.

It was decided to conduct the experiment in the school systems of Rochester, Detroit, Chicago, Kansas City, Denver, Los Angeles, San Diego, New York, Atlanta, Winston-Salem, and Newton, Massachusetts. The Eastman Kodak Company would provide a 16mm Kodascope projector to each school. Dr. Thomas E. Finnegan was appointed to direct the project, beginning in January 1927. Twenty-two educational films were put into production, ten on geography, five each on health and general science, one on iron in the industrial progress of the United States, and one on the life of a New England fisherman. A further thirty films were planned for completion by the summer of 1927.

According to Arthur Edwin Krows,

To prepare the content of these additional ones, teachers of the various subjects to be presented were brought to a training school at the Rochester offices during the summer. There, under the direction of experts in visual education and especially of film practices, they were able to hold frequent conferences and review each stage of the work as it proceeded. The technical supervision of all these films was referred to Herford Tynes Cowling, well known producer of travelogues, one-time cinematographer to Burton Holmes.[8]

Between 1926 and 1928, more than 10,000 students in the fourth, fifth, and sixth elementary grades and at the junior high school level were introduced to films as a regular part of their educational curriculum. Working under Dr. Finnegan in bringing the project to a successful conclusion were two professors, Dr. Ben Wood of Columbia University and Dr. Frank Freeman of the University of Chicago.

In 1928, the project ceased to be experimental; and Eastman Teaching Films, Inc., was incorporated with Dr. Finnegan as its president and general manager. The company began an active production and distribution program. Advertisements similar to the following were placed in all educational periodicals:

The hundred teachers whose pupils had the benefit of *Eastman Classroom Films* in the great experiment of 1928 are overwhelmingly convinced of their effectiveness. So are those who are using them now. Because: 1. These films arouse and maintain great interest. 2. They increase the quantity and improve the quality of reading, project work, classroom discussion and writing. 3. They help pupils to correlate materials more thoroughly. 4. They increase the richness, accuracy and meaningfulness of experience. 5. They facilitate the teacher's work of organizing lesson materials, and add to the pleasure and interest of teaching.[9]

The incorporation of the project did not halt the experiments. If anything, it encouraged company personnel to further efforts to prove the value of *Eastman Classroom Films*. In 1929, the company conducted a tenweek test with 11,000 children and 232 teachers in twelve cities. Fiftyfive hundred pupils were taught with the aid of the *Eastman Classroom Films*. They gained higher grades of 33 percent more in geography and 15 percent more in general science compared to an equal number of children taught without visual aids.

Aside from its work in the classroom, Eastman Teaching Films also became involved in the production of films for the medical community. At the 1926 Montreal convention of the American College of Physicians and Surgeons, Will H. Hays gave an address as honorary chairman of the College's committee to study the use of film. Hays arranged a meeting with representatives of Eastman Teaching Films, and as a result two films, *Infections of the Hand* and *Nursing*, were screened at the 1927 convention in Detroit. It was agreed that Eastman Teaching Films would produce films on anatomy, physiology, bacteriology, embryology, surgery, experimental medicine, health examination, obstetrics, hygiene, sanitation, public health, neurology, hospital practice, and nursing, and that such films would be distributed by the company, for sale and rental to doctors, nurses, and hospitals only.

Production of the original series of *Eastman Classroom Films* ceased in July 1932. In November of the same year Dr. Finnegan, who was still heading the company, died. In 1933, Eastman Teaching Films, Inc., was absorbed by the parent company, which became the Teaching Films Division of the Eastman Kodak Company. (The latter should not be confused with Teaching Films, Inc., founded in New York early in 1947.)

Of course, Eastman Kodak was active in a number of other areas of non-theatrical filmmaking. Aside from the Teaching Films Division, it operated an Informational Films Division. In 1963, in cooperation with CINE and the University Film Producers Association, Eastman Kodak sponsored a moviemaking contest for American teenagers. From 1950 until 1971, when he took an early retirement at the age of sixty-one, John Flory was Eastman Kodak's Advisor on Nontheatrical Films.

Flory graduated from Yale in 1932 and was involved in various aspects of film production before joining Eastman Kodak; he produced trailers for Paramount Pictures in Hollywood, headed his own sponsored film production company, Standard Films, and moved to New York in the late 1930s to form Grant, Flory, and Williams. John Flory's last production company was Flory Films, from which he decided to join Eastman Kodak in part because of business problems created by the Korean War. Flory's wife, Elizabeth (Bee) Harding Flory, was instrumental in the creation of the Educational Film Library Association.

In 1954, Thomas W. Hope joined Eastman Kodak as Assistant Advisor for Nontheatrical Films. After writing a number of definitions of the non-theatrical film for various dictionaries, the pair decided to drop the hyphen from the term, one of the reasons why the Council on International Nontheatrical Events is so named.

Four years after joining Eastman Kodak, Hope worked with Flory in the preparation of a report on the economic impact of the non-theatrical film industry. The report was published by the Society of Motion Picture and Television Engineers and proved so valuable that it became an annual publication, so popular by 1969 that 17,000 reprints were sold. That same year, Eastman Kodak decided to discontinue the reports. Rather than witness the death of the project, Thomas Hope left Eastman Kodak in April 1970, and with his wife founded Hope Reports, Inc., which published its first effort, *Hope Reports AV-USA 1969* in September 1970. Hope Reports provides data and information for the media communications industry, documenting media market trends, surveying product sales and services, and the like. The publication continues to be widely used for information as varied as national and regional wages and salaries, corporate spending on audiovisual production, employee productivity, and the number of producers in each major U.S. city.

Important as Eastman Kodak's many projects were, ultimately it is the introduction of 16mm film that makes the company pre-eminent in the evolution of non-theatrical filmmaking. Celebrating the twenty-fifth anniversary of home movies in the summer of 1948, *Film News* commented:

> Kodak set the 16mm size as standard—and insisted on safety film. This size precluded any splitting of 35mm nitrate films into widths for home use and thus removed a possible serious safety hazard.
>
> The company introduced an improved reversal process into the United States which perhaps more than any other one factor contributed to the swift growth of these movies.
>
> Kodak set up a worldwide system of processing stations.
>
> These steps "made" 16mm photography. They created an everyday event from what, previously, had been an oddity. In short, Eastman did for this field what his Kodak Camera did for amateur still photography—introduced it to the people as a whole and placed it within their financial means.[10]

NOTES

1. "Willard Cook: Father of Non-Theatrical in the U.S.A.," *Film News*, vol. VIII, no. 12 (June–July 1948), p. 5.

2. The agreement is in the Warner Bros. Collection at the Doheny Memorial Library of the University of Southern California.

3. Memorandum to Mr. Bandy from Mrs. Price, August 15, 1929, in Warner Bros. Collection (see note 2).

4. David Pierce, "Silent Movies and the Kodascope Libraries," *American Cinematographer*, vol. LXX, no. 1 (January 1989), p. 37.

5. Quoted in Douglas Collins, *The Story of Kodak* (New York: Harry N. Abrams, 1990), p. 188.

6. Carl W. Ackerman, *George Eastman* (Boston: Houghton Mifflin, 1930), p. 454.

7. *School and Society*, vol. XXIII, no. 586 (March 20, 1926), p. 358.

8. Arthur Edwin Krows, "Motion Pictures—Not for Theatres," *Educational Screen*, vol. XXI, no. 8 (October 1942), p. 304.

9. *Educational Screen*, vol. VIII, no. 3 (March 1929), p. 89.

10. "Kodak's 16mm History—From Lab to World Use," *Film News*, vol. VIII, no. 12 (June–July 1948), p. 7.

FOUR

Specialization

With the 35mm theatrical film industry devoted to entertainment for profit, it was left to the non-theatrical community to specialize in specific areas within the educational and industrial fields. Possibly the first area of specialization was medicine, with the cinema, early in its development, proving to be valuable in both documenting surgical procedures and making the work of specialists more readily available for study.

As early as 1902, the British company Urban Eclipse provided footage of surgical operations for study at the University of Birmingham. By 1908, the use of motion pictures to document the work of surgeons had become almost commonplace. In its issue for April 18, 1909, the trade paper *The Moving Picture World* reported, "In one of the New York hospitals moving pictures have been made of epileptic patients, as well as of persons affected with locometer ataxia. This is following the example set in Vienna, where moving pictures have been made of celebrated surgeons performing critical operations." At London's Middlesex Hospital, Dr. H. C. Thompson had arranged for the routine filming of surgical procedures, and films of operations were screened for students at Chicago's Night University.

Aside from their importance as documentation, films of surgical experiments might also help in the partial elimination of animal vivisection. Writing in 1928 in *Taking the Doctor's Pulse* ("dedicated to the most potent implement of modern education the Motion Picture Film"), J. F. Montague explained, "the trained physiologist does the experiment in an expert manner and its recording upon the film makes it repeatedly available at many times and in many places without the repetition of the experiment at the cost of other animal lives."[1]

Health education films date back at least to 1922, when the Metropolitan Life Insurance Company produced *One Scar or Many*, advocating vaccination against smallpox. Suture manufacturer Davis & Geck produced a series of films in the early 1930s, by which time some fourteen companies were reported to be specializing in medical films.[2] The first Medical Motion Picture Workshop was organized by the Calvin Company in Kansas City, from February 4 to February 6, 1957. That same year, the first International Medical Film Exhibition was held in New York, from June 3 to June 7, presented by the American Medical Association in cooperation with Johnson & Johnson.

In 1917 a conference of the American College of Surgeons advocated the use of motion pictures to standardize surgical procedures and thus lead to more efficient methods of surgery. At a January 1919 meeting, Major E. Tunstall Taylor of the Surgeon-General's Office commented:

> As a supervising surgeon, it early became apparent to me that simply the verbal lecture, with the limitations of the human voice and the absence of illustrations or clinical material, was inadequate for attention and retention by the memory; charts and slides were impractical; so that the moving pictures, on my initiative and the hearty cooperation of Colonel Owen, was established in the Surgeon-General's Office. . . . In creating these lectures, I have had in mind not only military instruction, but adding teaching facilities available for use in our civil medical schools. . . . The moving picture is very broadening in its educational possibilities.[3]

Since 1926, the American College of Surgeons has offered advice in the production of appropriate films, reviewing and evaluating them. Those which meet the college's basic standards are noted as "Passed by the Committee on Medical Motion Pictures of the American College of Surgeons." However, despite such an early interest in film as a teaching aid, it was not until 1955 that the College of Surgeons approved the creation of a film library. That same year it entered into an agreement with Davis & Geck for the production of between eighteen and twenty films a year.

Kings College Hospital began producing teaching films in 1930. Such films became part of the Kodak Medical Film Library, which within a few years numbered some 250 titles. In January 1935, Dr. Jacob Sarnoff announced that he had developed a surgical film library of over two hundred 400 ft. reels of 16mm film, covering more than 300 operations that he had performed.[4] In March 1936, *The Educational Screen* carried an advertisement for the Chicago-based Tate Animated Surgical Films, a

16mm library of one-reel subjects. The American Medical Association was somewhat late in acknowledging the value of medical films; it did not appoint a committee to promote their use until the spring of 1946, at which time it also announced plans to review such films in its journal. Two years later, the Royal Society of Medicine and the Scientific Film Association published its first catalog of medical films.

Following in the footsteps of the AMA, the first Audio Visual Conference of Medical and Allied Sciences was held in 1953, with participating representatives from the American Dental Association, the American Hospital Association, the American Medical Association, the American Veterinary Medical Association, and the Medical Audio-Visual Institute of the Association of American Medical Colleges. The last was the sponsor, that same year, of the book-length study, *Films in Psychiatry, Psychology & Mental Health.*[5]

While it was primarily doctors who first utilized the motion picture as an educational source, the nursing community eventually recognized the value of the medium in 1948, when Kathryn Linden established a film library at the American Nurses Association. In 1953, the library became the American Nurses Association/National League for Nursing Film Service. In 1970, by which time it held 1,419 prints of 97 films, the library was transferred to the American Journal of Nursing Company as its Educational Services Division.

It might appear somewhat surprising that the other major area of specialization in the non-theatrical film should be farming and agriculture, but it would seem less so if one is aware that one of the earliest industrial films dealt with the subject, and the first U.S. government department to become actively involved in filmmaking was the Department of Agriculture.

The department acquired the first 35mm motion picture camera to be owned by the federal government in 1908. It was not used to film an agricultural project but was used by Lewis Williams, chief of the division of illustrations, and his assistant, W. S. Cline, to film the Wright Brothers demonstrating a biplane at Fort Myers for the Army Signal Corps. A couple of years later, the camera was used again to photograph cattle shipments for Joseph Abel of the Bureau of Animal Industry and also to photograph U.S. Secretary of Agriculture James Wilson. The latter had not been supportive of the use of film, but when he was shown the footage, apparently taken by film and television pioneer C. Francis Jenkins, Wilson was won over to the cause; in 1912 he approved of Paul Reddington of the U.S. Forest Service accompanying an Edison cameraman on a filming expedition in the Sierras.

The Motion Picture Service at the U.S. Department of Agriculture was formalized in 1912, when a film laboratory was set up in the charge of W. S. Cline and George R. Georgens, working under the supervision of Andre Boetcher, chief of the section of illustrations. The laboratory was the first established by the government, and for more than sixty years was the only one under federal control. A departmental motion picture committee was formed in 1915, and by the following year it was able to ship forty films to the Panama–Pacific International Exposition in San Francisco.

The Motion Picture Service was headed from 1917 to 1919 by Don Carlos Ellis, and he moved away from non-theatrical film production, finding theatrical audiences for Department of Agriculture films by including them as episodes in short subject interest compilations and also by signing a distribution arrangement with Universal. In 1921, the Motion Picture Service was renamed the Office of Motion Pictures, and in 1924 it began production of a series of short subjects in cooperation with Pathé. As of 1925, it was reported that the Department of Agriculture held a library of 1,862 reels. The importance of the Office of Motion Pictures was emphasized in 1929 when it was made a full division of the Department of Agriculture. That same year the department produced its first "talkies."

The attitude of the department had always been that it was producing films to document a process or educate an audience. Writing of Robert Flaherty's classic 1934 documentary, Raymond Evans, then-chief of the Division of Motion Pictures, Extension Service, commented, "*Man of Aran* is no more 'documentary' than is the Moonlight Sonata. It is a poem in pictures, while some of the uninspiring but necessary films that *we* make are perhaps the true documentary pictures—if we *must* use that word."[6] One film that did not fit Evans' definition was *Power and the Land*, directed in 1940 by renowned documentary filmmaker Pare Lorentz to illustrate the value of rural electrification to the American farmer. This and two other government-sponsored films produced by Lorentz, *The Plow That Broke the Plains* (1937) and *The River* (1938), were influential in the establishment, by President Franklin Delano Roosevelt, of the U.S. Film Service in 1938.

The facilities of the Motion Picture Division were taken over during the Second World War by the Office of Strategic Services, but at the conclusion of hostilities the Department of Agriculture was back in film production again. So prominent had the department's work become that in 1962, to highlight the centennial year of the department's foundation, a Film Festival of Agriculture was organized.[7]

No company was as important as International Harvester in pioneering the use of sponsored production and film as an advertising medium. Founded in 1902 by Cyrus McCormick, the International Harvester Company quickly became the world's leading manufacturer of farm equipment, revolutionizing American agriculture. It was also to help revolutionize the non-theatrical film industry through its early recognition of the sponsored film as a unique method of self-promotion and advertising.

In 1909, the company produced a series of films, under the title "The Romance of the Reaper," that were screened in theatres accompanied by pre-set and company-approved lectures by George Frederick Wheeler and others. Writing in *The Nickelodeon* (January 1909), Wilson Mayer commented, "Nothing can equal in interest the actual living reproduction on the screen of the real scenes of gigantic agricultural industry. The waving grain, ripening under the clear skies and beneficent sunshine of the great Northwest; the vast accomplishment of the marvelous machinery designed by man to do more and better work than man himself could do; the great granaries rapidly filling with the great foundations of the staff of life; all these things are presented to the spectator in their ideal form."

Three years later, International Harvester sponsored the production of *Back to the Old Farm*, released by the General Film Company on September 3, 1912. One reel in length, the film was produced by the Essanay Film Manufacturing Company and shot at its Chicago studio and on location in Wayne, Illinois. Starring Essanay's best-known leading lady, Beverly Bayne, supported by William Bailey, E. H. Calvert, Frank Dayton, and Lily Branscombe, the film was written by E. L. Barker and supervised by Frank W. Heiskell.

Reviewing *Back to the Old Farm* on September 7, 1912, *The Moving Picture World* made no mention of International Harvester's sponsorship of the production:

> This is a charming summer pastoral story, unique in plot conception and showing the most modern farming methods as compared with those of years gone by, and has been splendidly portrayed by the Essanay Eastern players. . . .
>
> The Essanay Company have succeeded in making a thoroughly pleasing production of this unique story. The scenes about the old fashioned farm with everything in confusion at the beginning of the film are characteristic and absolutely true to life, while the later views of the modern farm with all its fine machinery and conveniences, and showing just how the appliances are used, are of great educational value to all who view the photoplay.

The film's plot line is easily discernible through *Back to the Old Farm's* original titles:

1. George receives an invitation to spend his vacation on the old farm.
2. That night he dreams of the drudgery of farming as he knew it.
3. He recalls the labor of picking up the grain cut by the early reaper.

4. Of the nuisance of unhitching, feeding and watering a team of horses.

5. On his return he surprises his boyhood sweetheart, Beverly Bayne.

6. She shows him how new machinery has taken the drudgery from farming.

7. A modern gas engine generates current to separate milk and churn butter.

8. An auto wagon, early International truck, hauls passengers and produce.

9. Childhood sweethearts, they elope in the farm's modern carriage.

10. The mailman's International truck brings news of the happy finale!

In 1940, sound was added to *Back to the Old Farm*, and it was reissued as a comedy.

In 1952, the old Essanay studios were utilized by Wilding Picture Productions for the filming of a new International Harvester film, *Inside Harvester, U.S.A.*, a 55-minute Kodachrome feature. International Harvester produced its first comedy, a one-reeler titled *Farm Inconveniences*, written by Ralph A. Hayne, in 1916. Its first sound film, with sound-on-disc, was *Romance of the Reaper* in 1931; and the company's first sound-on-film production came in 1934 with *Farmall Farming Marches On*.

As of 1948, the International Harvester Company had thirty-seven films in circulation, all distributed out of its Chicago headquarters, of which twenty-seven were educational, seven were industrial, and three were comedies. They varied in length from one to three reels and covered subjects as diverse as soil conservation, farm safety, and rural schools. International Harvester's marketing of its new films was as revolutionary as its initial entry into the field. The company sponsored annual power-farming "entertainments" around the country; they were old-fashioned parties to which the entire farming community was invited to preview the latest releases.

The International Harvester Company relied on a variety of production houses for the creation of its films. Of its five releases in the 1950s, *It's Still up to You* (1955) and *Out of This World* (1955) were produced by Vogue Wright Studios, *Day in Court* (1951) was produced by Cate & McGlone, *Inside Harvester, U.S.A.* (1952) was produced by Wilding Picture Productions, and *Man with a Thousand Hands* (1953) was an internal production.

Prior to the financial losses of the 1970s and 1980s, which ultimately led to International Harvester's reorganization on February 10, 1986, as Navistar International Corp., the company continued in film sponsorship, with one of its last releases being *News and Views in Agriculture* in 1972, intended for use by its franchised farm equipment dealers.

Another early film sponsor from the agricultural community was the

Caterpillar Tractor Company, formed in 1925 through the merger of the Holt Manufacturing Co. and the C. L. Best Tractor Co. One of the predecessor companies produced a 1916 short subject dealing with the work of U.S. farmers in the production of vital food supplies during wartime. Caterpillar produced its first sound film in 1932 and its first color release in 1939. All in all, between 1939 and 1941 its advertising department wrote, prepared, and edited some fourteen films. "They are in no sense Hollywood productions," commented *Business Screen*. "They are simply demonstrations of what the machines will do on many types of work."[8]

Deere and Company began film sponsorship in 1930. It was later joined by other companies, including the American Feed Manufacturers Association, American Plant Food Council, Associated Serum Producers, Inc., and American Agricultural Chemical Company.

The first attempt to form an organization to distribute films as teaching aids for farmers came in July 1921, when the Farm Films Service was established by the Chicago-based American Farm Bureau, in collaboration with the Illinois Agricultural Association. With funding in large part from the Foundation for American Agriculture, the Farm Film Foundation, Inc., was founded in May 1946 to bring educational films to rural America, through screenings to 4-H Clubs, Future Farmers of America, and like organizations. In 1948 it became self-supporting from the fees paid by sponsors for the distribution of their films and consultation services provided to producers.

In 1950, *Business Screen* commented,

> The people who have struggled to build the Foundation into an institution with fourteen major branches scattered across the country and seven additional sub-branches showing to audiences in strictly rural America of approximately 2,000,000 gaze back with a feeling of wonder and amazement at how far the Foundation has come in such a short time. With the experience they now have accumulated, they are looking forward to an ever-increasing number of good pictures and an ever-increasing audience in rural America. They believe they are working with the most important media available to unite our American people in our fight to survive in a chaotic world.[9]

The Farm Film Foundation was renamed the Grange-Farm Film Foundation in 1980. At the time of its demise in 1988, the foundation maintained a library of 3,200 films, videotapes, and slide sets and published an annual catalog of 16mm films.

Specialization in subject matter was matched by the variety of venues for the burgeoning non-theatrical film industry. Schools and churches were obvious prime locations, but many other less-apparent exhibition sites were discovered by the industry. In-flight movies today are an important outgrowth of the non-theatrical film industry, although now utilizing videotapes rather than films; the term is a misnomer. Yet in-flight movies were once a novelty, growing from an earlier use of films to entertain riders on passenger trains. Similarly, non-theatrical screen-ings in prisons, hospitals, and elsewhere are examples of the never-ending search by an industry anxious to locate new markets for its product.

Open-air screenings date back at least to August 1917, when educa-tional films were shown three nights a week, free of charge, in the public parks of Schenectady, New York. "The films will be purely educational and will deal with travel, industry and manufacture," reported the *New York Dramatic Mirror* (July 28, 1917), anxious to placate the city's theatre owners, who might regard such presentations as unfair competition. No doubt as a partial response to such summertime open-air screenings, drive-in movie theatres were introduced on a regular basis beginning in 1933; but they are, of course, theatrical settings. An experiment that does not appear to have been repeated was the screening of Goldwyn feature films for diners on Wednesday and Saturday evenings at the Arrowhead Hotel in Arrowhead Springs, California, in June 1918. It was reported that more than 2,000 visitors saw the first two presentations of *Polly of the Circus*, featuring Mae Marsh, and *Baby Mine*, starring Madge Kennedy.

In theory, screenings in restaurants should have gone out of favor with the coming of sound, as "talkies" could not possibly compete with the noise of the diners; but there were in fact continued attempts to present films at eating establishments. In 1931, "The Talky Sandwich Shop" opened in San Diego, and throughout the 1930s there were ex-perimental screenings of films in bars and grills. Some states even tried to regulate the novelty.

In recent years the use of comedy and animated shorts at fast-food establishments catering to children has been tried with moderate suc-cess. The screening of appropriate features at "gay bars" throughout the United States had some popularity in the 1970s and early 1980s but slowly died out, in part because the screenings were a violation of copy-right laws that could result in harassment of the bar owners by the Federal Bureau of Investigation.

Office and factory workers have been subjected to film screenings during their lunch breaks, sometimes for entertainment but generally for informational and educational reasons. During the Second World War, the Electro-Motive Division of General Motors screened 16mm films in the employee cafeteria during lunch hours. In 1960, the John Hancock Mutual Life Insurance Company was offering free films for its employees at noon each day. There are probably countless other examples of the practice.

The earliest-known screening on an ocean liner in American waters was on the Italian ship, *Duca d'Aosta*, in July 1914. Films were shown to first-class passengers five nights a week, and twice weekly in second class. French ocean liners appear to have offered films for transatlantic passengers in 1912, with the Hamburg-America line adopting the practice the following year. For reasons of fire safety, the screening of nitrate films on American ocean liners was banned until 1923. The ban did not apply to ships of the U.S. Navy; and by September 1923, *The Educational Screen* was able to report that the Brooklyn Navy Yard "has one of the largest film exchanges in the world."[10] In fact, the non-theatrical presentation of films to the U.S. armed forces dates back at least to 1913. On March 19 of that year, the Nicholas Power Company placed an advertisement in the *New York Dramatic Mirror* announcing that its Power's Cameragraph No. 6a Projector was in use at thirty army posts and battleships.

The popular notion of screening films as part of an educational cruise dates back to 1929, when the American Institute of Educational Travel organized a Mediterranean cruise on the Cunard and Anchor liner *California*.

In 1914, the Chicago and Northwestern Railroad began screening movies on some of its passenger runs, and the following year Kinetic Films was founded in Buffalo, New York, to supply films to passenger trains. In 1947, the Chesapeake and Ohio Railway introduced "the Chessie Theatre," a 16mm film theatre in a converted dining car, as a regular feature on its Newport News to Cincinnati run. The first presentation was the world premiere of Universal-International's *Swell Guy*, directed by Frank Tuttle and starring Sonny Tufts and Ann Blythe. Universal-International provided all of the films utilized by the railroad.

An even more unusual location for a non-theatrical screening was a Los Angeles streetcar on which, in December 1929, the Harold Lloyd feature *Safety Last* was presented. Some fifty years later, in the winter of 1979–1980, passengers traveling on the San Francisco Municipal Railway were treated to experimental video presentations created by Armin Ganz and promoted as "Munimovies."

The first American in-flight movie presentation is believed to have been that of a Universal newsreel and two short subjects on a transcontinental Air Transport, Inc., Ford Transport, on October 8, 1929. According to *Motion Picture Herald*, the documentary feature *Baboona* was previewed on board a plane in December 1934; and the film's producers, Mr. and Mrs. Martin Johnson, announced their intention of outfitting one of their planes with a sound projector in order to screen the film for African natives (who represented the cast of the feature) in the summer of 1935. As a publicity stunt, the 1933 Columbia feature *Air Hostess* (directed by Al Rogell and starring Thelma Todd and James Murray) was screened for reporters in an airplane flying over New York in the fall of 1936. Early in 1946, Pan-Am tested the screening of films on its North Atlantic run and in the fall of that year announced that 16mm films would be shown on transoceanic flights on a regular basis. The films were provided by Seven Seas Film Corporation, which had been founded in the late 1930s by Orton Hicks and Earle W. Carder to service the needs of clients in the transportation field; it was later merged with Modern Film Corp. and renamed Movies Enroute, Inc.

The first airline to introduce and maintain regular in-flight presentations was TWA, beginning on July 19, 1961, with *By Love Possessed*, directed by John Sturges and featuring Lana Turner and Efrem Zimbalist, Jr.

The attempt by Osa and Martin Johnson to screen films for African natives was far from being the earliest use of non-theatrical films on the African continent. Missionaries had early recognized the potential of the motion picture. In *Motion Picture Classic* (June 1916), Ernest A. Dench wrote,

> The modern method of educating heathens is by Motion Pictures. With the able assistance of a fairly durable projection machine and a collection of suitable films, the missionary can do much to convert them to Christianity. . . .
>
> In the days before Christianity, the recognized thought transference medium, so we are led to believe, was to cut crude pictures on slabs of stone. The modern equivalent of this is the Motion Picture. The eye can absorb much which the brain cannot. Imagine, then, the effect such a classic as *From the Manger to the Cross* [1912] would have on heathens out in Africa or the South Seas. Would not the life of our Savior impress them to a favorable degree? There are many Biblical stories which could bring home to them the foolishness of worshiping stone and wooden idols.
>
> Educational films, on the other hand, would afford them a comprehensive insight into how the Christian world lives today. American cities, industries, customs and sanitation are some of the subjects which are eminently suited for the purpose.

It is not possible to document the first time that films were screened in American prison facilities. It is known that a feature titled *The Ninety and Nine* (Vitagraph, 1916) was shown at the county jail in Scranton, Pennsylvania, on December 25, 1916, and that films were screened at Sing Sing in February of the following year. There was limited screening of films for allied prisoners during the First World War, and even at the Buchenwald concentration camp in 1944. War Prisoners Aid and the YMCA arranged for the screening of 16mm films to U.S. prisoners of war in German-occupied territories during the Second World War. According to *Business Screen*, "Through camp movie shows American prisoners are able to turn their minds away from the dreary routine of confinement. The music and comedy of the outside world, the familiar faces and scenes of home—these contributions of the screen, observers say, do much to keep their spirits up and relieve the monotony of the endless days."[11]

In the early 1970s, the American Film Institute attempted to interest the general public in film preservation through the presentation of special screenings at selected department stores. The idea was not new. Films of fashion shows were presented at Harris–Emery's Department Store in Des Moines in September 1916. In 1929, the Home–Talkie Machine Corporation marketed a sound film of Santa Claus, which was utilized by a number of department stores.

The use of films for political purposes has its origins in one of the first public presentations of the new medium. Among the original American Biograph productions shown at Hammerstein's Olympia Theatre in New York in October 1896 were two glimpses of the Republican nominee for president, William McKinley. According to the *New York Dramatic Mirror* (October 24, 1896), "The house was crowded and the picture of McKinley set the audience wild. Seldom is such a demonstration seen in a theatre. The entire audience rose to their feet, shouting and waving American flags, and it was several minutes before they settled down quietly to enjoy the rest of the performance." It was perhaps no coincidence that present in the audience were several prominent Republicans, including vice presidential nominee Garret Hobart.

McKinley might have been the first American president to be on film, except that his predecessor Grover Cleveland was present when the cameras filmed the former's inauguration in March 1897. McKinley was filmed quite extensively—for example, in 1901 the Edison Company released *President McKinley's Speech at the Pan-Pacific Exposition* and *President McKinley Taking the Oath*—as were his successors, Roosevelt and Taft. Woodrow Wilson was, arguably, the first American president to understand the propaganda value of the motion picture. Calvin Coolidge was the first president to make a sound speech for the motion picture, on his economic policies in 1924.

President Franklin D. Roosevelt displayed sophistication in his use of the film industry to promote his policies; for example, in 1934 Roosevelt's National Recovery Administration sponsored a short subject titled *The Road Is Open Again*, in which Dick Powell spoke with the ghosts of Washington, Lincoln, and Wilson and sang of the bright future offered by the NRA. Roosevelt also found a more insidious use for the motion picture. Shortly after he had established the Office of War Information on June 13, 1942, it produced *Japanese Relocation*, which attempted to justify the incarceration of Americans of Japanese descent by showing "the standard that we are setting for the rest of the world in the treatment of people who may have loyalties to an enemy nation."

One of the earliest surviving films promoting the election of a president is *A Musical Message from Hollywood*, which urges Roosevelt to run for a third term. Directed by two Hollywood leftists, Herbert Biberman and Frank Tuttle, the short subject features Charles Purcell singing "Mr. Roosevelt Won't You Do It Again," while the viewers see what is presumably a typical Hollywood liberal's home, complete with swimming pool and happy workers and sited directly under the Hollywood Sign.[12]

In 1958, the League of Women Voters acknowledged the value of the motion picture with the publication of the first edition of *Leading Film Discussions*. "A film attracts people to a meeting," explained the League, "and when followed by a sharing of reactions, it changes an audience into a group."[13]

There have been several early examples of the attempted judicial use of films. In March 1923, Judge Weil of the Manhattan Domestic Relations Court "projected for the benefit of an exceptional number of men and women before him who were in marital difficulties, a theatrical motion picture which, in his opinion, dealt constructively with the subject of bickering couples."[14] It was an unusual move in that more often than not courts had ruled against the use of films. As early as February 1920, a California court refused to allow motion pictures to be used as murder evidence, and a similar ruling was handed down in November 1923 by a New York court in an accident suit. These decisions notwithstanding, in 1929 police in Philadelphia used film to record a murder conviction.

One of the first uses by the police of film as a public relations tool came in 1905, when New York Police Commissioner William McAdoo authorized Roundsman Daniel J. Fogarty to negotiate with F. F. Proctor's Enterprises for the production of a film on the life of a New York policeman. "The picture idea is an admirable one," wrote McAdoo, "particularly as the case of Patrolman Enright was enacted, along with the chasing of the thief, the killing of Enright, the wounding of Patrolman Bachman and, finally, the capture of the thief. I believe also that the scene of a patrolman rescuing a man or woman from drowning would appeal very strongly to the public and show forcibly the courage and bravery of the men who make up this force."[15]

Eighty-six years later, the Los Angeles Police Department was confronted with a videotape record of the vicious beating of an unarmed black man by a dozen of their number.[16] The years roll by, the medium changes from film to videotape, and new specialized non-theatrical uses continue to be discovered.

NOTES

1. J. F. Montague, *Taking the Doctor's Pulse* (Philadelphia: J. B. Lippincott, 1928), p. 43.

2. "The Film in Medicine," *Business Screen*, vol. XIII, no. 6 (September 28, 1952), pp. 27–29.

3. Quoted in Dr. Malcolm T. MacEachern, "War Medicine and the Screen," *Business Screen*, vol. IV, no. 2 (March 1, 1942), p. 14.

4. Dr. Jacob Sarnoff, "The Cinema in Surgery," *Educational Screen*, vol. XIV, no. 1 (January 1935), pp. 9–10, 22–23.

5. Adolf Nichtenhauser, Marie L. Coleman, and David S. Ruhe, *Films in Psychiatry, Psychology & Mental Health* (New York: Health Education Council, 1953).

6. Raymond Evans, "The Motion Picture Policy of the United States Department of Agriculture," *Educational Screen*, vol. XVI, no. 9 (November 1937), p. 284.

7. Much of the information on the film activities of the Department of Agriculture is taken from Arthur Edwin Krows, "Motion Pictures—Not for Theatres," *Educational Screen*, vol. XXI, no. 1 (January 1942), pp. 14–17, 21; and from "Agriculture on Film," *Film News*, vol. XIX, no. 5 (November–December 1952), pp. 6–7, 23.

8. *Business Screen*, vol. III, no. 5 (May 17, 1941), p. 28.

9. "Farm Film Foundation Gains Stature," *Business Screen*, vol. XI, no. 4 (June 26, 1950), p. 31.

10. *Educational Screen*, vol. II, no. 7 (September 1923), p. 367.

11. "Prisoners See Features," *Business Screen*, vol. VI, no. 2 (December 30, 1944), p. 42.

12. *A Musical Message from Hollywood* is safeguarded by the UCLA Film and Television Archive.

13. *Leading Film Discussions: A Guide to Using Films for Discussion, Training Leaders, Planning Effective Programs* (New York: League of Women Voters, 1972), p. 1.

14. Arthur Edwin Krows, "Motion Pictures—Not for Theatres," *Educational Screen*, vol. XXII, no. 1 (January 1943), p. 15.

15. Letter dated September 19, 1905, in the author's possession.

16. The implication of easy access to a home video camera is discussed in "Video Vigilantes," *Newsweek*, July 22, 1991, pp. 42–47.

FIVE

Film in Education and Religion

Despite Thomas Edison's advocacy of film as an educational force, educators and others were slow to recognize and act upon its potential; in part because of the many perceived negative aspects of the medium. Community groups were generally alert to the danger that the cinema would pervert young minds but slow to acknowledge its potential for good.

In September 1914, Orrin G. Cocks, secretary of the National Board of Censorship, wrote in *Library Journal*, "The libraries of the United States have failed to see the educational value of motion pictures during their period of growth in the last 15 years."[1] Cocks pointed out that at least six models of 35mm projectors could be purchased "for a price around $100."[2] He named seven film companies with active libraries of educational films: The General Film Company, Pathé Freres, Eclair, the Thomas A. Edison Company, Gaumont, George Kleine, and the Hepworth American Film Corporation. Further, Cocks pointed out that at least three agencies existed to service the need of libraries for film: the Community Service & Film Bureau (headed by the Rev. Charles Stelze), the Church and School Social Service (headed by the Rev. William Carter), and the Motion Picture Bureau (headed by Edward W. Robinson).

Some twelve years later, Melvil Dewey, the first secretary of the Amer-

ican Library Association, used the pages of *Library Journal* again to urge
that librarians embrace film:

> Will Hays published the other day his report on the movie theatre—
> twenty-three thousand of them with ninety million people attending them
> every week, with an income of a thousand million dollars each year and
> growing rapidly. If you can carry information or inspiration or recreation
> to human beings better or quicker or cheaper, the librarian is bound to
> use that means. . . .
>
> If the movies are teaching so many million a week not to read, let us
> utilize that great means, for the motion picture, decried and abused by
> every man, is one of the greatest agencies for education man has yet
> devised. A bad book is as efficient for evil as a good book is for good.[3]

Libraries began to acknowledge the value of film as early as 1920,
when the Milwaukee Public Library established a film department. Ka-
lamazoo followed in 1929, but it was a decade or more before most
libraries created audiovisual or film departments, making available educational (and sometimes entertainment) films to their patrons. Bertha
Landers (who founded *Landers Film & Video Reviews* in 1956) created an
audiovisual division at the Dallas Public Library in 1942; her example was
followed by Cleveland in 1943, Boston and Cincinnati in 1947, Rochester,
New York, in 1948, Los Angeles in 1951, and Brooklyn in 1952.

In April 1940, the Rockefeller Foundation made a grant of $5,500 to
the Visual Methods Committee (later the Audio-Visual Committee) of
the American Library Association to study the use of films within the
public library system. The committee, chaired by Mary U. Rothrock
(supervisor of the Library and Visual Education Service of the Tennessee
Valley Authority), hired Gerald Doan McDonald, chief of the Reserve
Room at the New York Public Library; he took a seven months' leave
of absence to prepare the study. (McDonald is better remembered today
as co-author of the 1965 Citadel Press book, *The Films of Charlie Chaplin*.)

McDonald's study was published by the American Library Association
in 1942 under the title *Educational Motion Pictures and Libraries*. It examined the Educational Film, Film and the Public Library, Films in Adult
Education, Films in the School Library, Films in the College and University Library, Films as Historical Records, and Training for Library
Film Service. McDonald noted, "If books were as hard to get as films,
little reading would be done in this country."[4] He urged the need for
more study and experimentation in "how to use films to greatest educational advantage, particularly in adult education, how to improve distribution and provide more 'personalized contact between producer or
distributor and the consumer,' and how to train librarians and educators
in the intricacies of bringing films into widespread and effective use for
educational ends."[5]

In arguing the need for films to be stocked in libraries in exactly the same manner as books were selected, McDonald also pleaded the need for the preservation of educational films as historical records and the urgent need for a ready supply of 16mm projectors within the country's public library system. The call for preservation of educational films still remains largely unheeded in the 1990s. The need for projectors illustrates a basic problem in comparing films to books. They are in no shape or form alike, in that films require machinery through which to come to life for their viewer/reader.

The American Library Association continued its interest in film and in 1947 was the recipient of a $27,000 grant from the Carnegie Corporation for the appointment of a full-time film advisor, Patricia Blair. Her appointment ended when the grant expired in 1951. Earlier, in February 1941, the Carnegie Corporation had made grant monies available for the creation by public libraries of film forums, at which film programs might be the subject of community discussion. The Washington, D.C., Film Council was established in 1943 as the Washington Visual War Workers Group, and it was followed by film councils in New York (1946) and Chicago (1947).

The last major effort to formalize the activities of librarians in the field of film distribution came on May 12, 1967, when the Film Library Information Council was founded at a meeting of film librarians from public libraries at the American Film Festival. The Council began publication of a journal, *Film Library Quarterly*, under the editorship of William Sloan in the winter of 1967–1968, which continued publication until 1984, when the journal was merged with *Sightlines*.[6] Another organization, the Cinema Librarians' Discussion Group, active in the 1970s and 1980s, was a loose-knit confederation of librarians involved with film literature rather than film per se.

The demise of *Film Library Quarterly* might be taken to mean the final curtain on audiovisual activities in public libraries, but rather such activities have been transferred from film to videotape; and in fact many public library systems have expanded their videotape loan operations to cover not only major libraries but also many small branch libraries, which would never have been considered as appropriate centers for film distribution. In an age when a videotape rental house has replaced the neighborhood grocery store as the most familiar sight at each street corner, the expansion of videotape rentals in the public library service might well be considered both unnecessary and unfair competition.

The use of audiovisual aids in education has its origins in the 1904 St. Louis World's Fair. As part of the exhibit, School Superintendent F. Louis Soldan, Assistant Superintendent Carl G. Rathmann, and teacher Miss Amelia Meissner created a living-school exhibit as part of the Fair's Palace of Education. Noticing the interest in the other attractions of the fair from the children participating in the living-school exhibit (which included two thousand photographs taken by Miss Meissner), Soldan and Rathmann were able to persuade various exhibitors to donate items such as lantern slides and photographs that might normally have been destroyed. These materials and a $1,000 grant from the Board of Education led to the creation of the School Museum, which opened on April 11, 1905. Miss Meissner, who might well be described as the mother of the audiovisual movement, was appointed the first head of the museum, which in 1943 was renamed the Division of Audio-Visual Education.

Aside from encouraging children to visit the museum, Miss Meissner also circulated exhibits to St. Louis schools, adopting the slogan, "Bring the World to the Child." Similar school museums were opened in Reading, Pennsylvania, in 1908 and in Cleveland, Ohio, in 1909. Together they mark the beginning of the audiovisual movement in American education, although film was markedly absent from the various artifacts in the museums. Educational films were not added to the collections of the St. Louis and Cleveland museums until 1923.[7]

In February 1910, Dr. William Henry Maxwell, superintendent of the New York Board of Education, announced his support for the use of films in the classroom. There was, without question, some limited use of film for educational purposes prior to 1910. The reason that the use was limited may not have been entirely a lack of interest but rather that films were 35mm and printed on highly flammable film stock. Access to portable projection equipment by school authorities was limited, and the fire risk was substantial. Certainly the commercial film production companies were aware of potential revenues from the educational use of their releases, and the leading film industry trade paper, *The Moving Picture World*, published a weekly "Educational Department."

In the *Moving Picture Annual and Yearbook for 1912*, the Reverend W. H. Jackson noted that "at the present time no thoroughly organized use has been made of the motion picture," but continued, "the world's educators, who are, as a class, slow to look upon any new thing, fearing it may be only of passing value, began to see in the moving picture possibilities that might be permanent, wide-spreading, and far-reaching, and determined to give it their warmest support."[8]

The annual included a ten-page listing of approximately 750 educational subjects released in 1912 under the following headings: General Topics, Religion, Moral Theology: Ethics, Sociology, Army and Navy: War, Social Life and Work, Science, Zoology, Industrial Arts and Sciences, Engineering, Agriculture, Domestic Economy and Commerce, Trades and Industries, Fine Arts, Literature, History, Geography, and Biography.

In 1914, schools in Georgia began to utilize films on a regular basis, and they were followed the next year by institutions in Ohio.

The 1920s were the decade of major expansion for educational film and its users. Following a plea by its president Will Hays for closer ties between educators and film producers, the Motion Picture Producers and Distributors Association provided a grant to F. Dean McClusky to survey the status of visual education. McClusky determined that there were 140 projectors in use in the New York City school system, 200 in Chicago, and 150 in Wisconsin. Further, administrators in Illinois, Texas, Philadelphia, and Newark were suggesting that projectors should be standard equipment in every one of the schools in their jurisdiction. Newark's Assistant Superintendent A. G. Balsom prepared a *Descriptive Classified Catalog of Educational Films for Classroom Use* in 1922.

A group of educators, primarily from the University of Chicago, got together and began publication of *The Educational Screen*, which explained in its first editorial, "This magazine intends to get at the truth about visual education—in all its phases and in its broadest aspects—and serve it up in a form palatable to thinking Americans."[9] As evidence of *The Educational Screen*'s growing importance as the primary source of information and discussion on the use of film in the classroom, in December 1922 it took over and combined with *The Moving Picture Age*, which had begun life as *Reel and Slide* and published under its new title since October 1918.

The Educational Screen further enhanced its position as the leading authority on the subject when, in April 1925, it merged with *Visual Education*. The latter had been published since January 1920, to service the motion picture needs of American schools, by the Society for Visual Education. Despite its name, the Society for Visual Education was a commercial venture founded in 1919 by Chicago public utilities tycoon Harley L. (Lyman) Clarke (1882–1955). Clarke invited a number of prominent educators to sit on the Society's board and embarked on an ambitious program of production of needed classroom films. Within two years, he had sixty titles in his catalog. Equally important, the Society for Visual Education marketed the first portable motion picture projector built specifically for classroom use; steel-cased and asbestos-lined, the "Acme" was a combination film and glass slide projector. In 1929, the Society for Visual Education was sold to Marie Witham and Bert Kleerup. Clarke moved into mainstream filmmaking, succeeding William Fox in what proved to be a financially disastrous presidency of the Fox Film Corporation in 1930.

The move to Fox did not mark the end of Clarke's interest in the educational film. In 1931, he decided to establish an educational film department at the studio, embarking on a series of productions under the title "Movietone School Series" at Fox's New York headquarters on West Fifty-fourth Street. The educational film department produced a two-reel subject on *The Educational Value of the Motion Picture*; various lecture reels featuring such well-known educators of the day as Wallace Atwood, Clyde Fisher, and Forest Ray Moulton; and even picked up an endorsement from President Herbert Hoover.

Additionally, the department made prints of older Fox features available for classroom use and created a new magazine-style short subject series, "The Magic Carpet of Movietone," photographed by Fox Movietone News cameramen. The entire project collapsed when Clarke was removed as Fox president. An attempt was made to save the department with the creation of a new, independent, non-profit organization to produce and distribute educational films, the International Film Foundation, headed by Dr. Atwood, but it collapsed also.

At the Society for Visual Education, Clarke's vice president and general manager was Nelson L. Greene (1881–1947). Greene was the first editor of *Visual Education*, but, disagreeing with Clarke, he resigned in the fall of 1921 and the following year became the first editor of *The Educational Screen*, a position he was to hold until his death.

The first managing editor of *The Educational Screen* was A. P. Hollis, who had founded the visual education department at North Dakota Agricultural College in 1918 and published an early text on classroom films, *Motion Pictures for Instruction*, in 1926. Hollis is almost completely forgotten, but something he wrote in 1920 remains in distribution today and familiar to anyone who has ever rented a 16mm film. It is "The Film Prayer," which Hollis neither copyrighted nor signed but made available for use by all non-theatrical film distributors as part of an effort to promote the better physical handling of film:

> I am celluloid, not steel; O God of the machine, have mercy. I front dangers whenever I travel the whirring wheels of the mechanism. Over the sprocket wheels, held tight by the idlers, I am forced by the motor's might. If a careless hand misthreads me, I have no alternative but to go to my death. If the pull on the take-up reel is too violent, I am torn to shreds. If dirt collects in the aperture, my film of beauty is streaked and marred, and I must face my beholders—a thing ashamed and bespoiled. I travel many miles in tin cans. I am tossed on heavy trucks, sideways and upside down. See that I don't become bruised and wounded beyond the power to heal. I am a delicate ribbon of film—misuse me and I disappoint thousands; cherish me, and I delight and instruct the world.

The 1920s saw the formation of an increasing number of organizations concerned with the educational use of motion pictures. In the fall of 1920, the Oklahoma Visual Education Association was founded, in cooperation with the Department of Visual Education at the University of Oklahoma. The Utah Visual Instruction Association was created in April 1922; three months later, on July 6, 1922, the Visual Instruction Association of America was organized in Boston, under the aegis of the

Division of Superintendents of the National Education Association. Its avowed purpose was to serve as a clearinghouse for ideas and information on visual aids to instruction.

The National Congress of Parents and Teachers had long been evaluating theatrical motion pictures. In September 1923, it took a look at *Human Wreckage*, produced by Mrs. Wallace Reid after the drug-induced death of her matinée idol husband, and recommended the feature "because it is said that the drug habit permeates our high schools." In the fall of 1924 that same viewing committee was incorporated as Film Councils of America. The recognition of film as an educational medium was further emphasized by the first major texts on the subject: *Motion Pictures in Education* by Don Carlos Ellis and Laura Thornborough (Thomas Y. Crowell, 1923) and *Visual Education: A Comparative Study of Motion Pictures and Other Methods of Instruction*, edited by Frank N. Freeman (University of Chicago Press, 1924).

What was to become one of the most prominent organizations in the field of audiovisual education, the Department of Audiovisual Instruction (DAVI) was founded in 1923 as the Department of Visual Instruction at an Oakland-San Francisco meeting of the National Education Association. An important rival group, the National Academy of Visual Instruction, was founded in 1927 as a Western group by William A. Dudley and an Eastern group by Ernest L. Crandall. The two divisions became one sometime between 1929 and 1931 and merged the following year with DAVI.[10]

In March 1928, *The Educational Screen* editorialized, "We believe that the incubation period for the visual movement is about over."[11] In reality, it would appear to have ended some eight years previously.

The coming of sound together with the more general availability of 16mm projection equipment increased the use of film in the classroom. Certainly sound films were slow at first to gain a hold in schools, in part because of the cost of installing new projection equipment and also because a sound-on-film 16mm projector was not available prior to 1932; but the advocates of motion pictures as teaching aids were steadily increasing in number, and they were being listened to. There were few arguments when Terry Ramsaye, the noted chronicler of film history whose 1926 text *A Million and One Nights* was to become a classic of film literature, wrote, "The educator must make the motion picture a tool in his own hands, and the man who can now write text books and deliver lectures, must come to consider the motion picture camera and the film as much their instrument as the typewriter, the printed press and the printed page—and, yes, the spoken word."[12]

The first American school equipped to screen "talkies"—utilizing a Western Electric 35mm portable sound system—was the Hotchkiss School at Lakeville, Connecticut, early in 1930. The first public school system to introduce sound motion pictures was that of Newark, New

Jersey, in April 1930; its first presentation was a subject with the formidable title, "*Administrative Departments of the Federal Government.*" Dr. Harry D. Kitson, professor of education at Teachers College, New York, prophesied that "beginning with the school year 1930–31, talking pictures will be adopted by some of our most progressive schools and colleges in an experimental way."[13]

A 1931 project sponsored by the U.S. Office of Education confirmed that the sound motion picture was "approximately twice as rich in instructional values as its silent predecessor." What the U.S. Office of Education ignored was that all the sound films available to schools up to that time were nothing more than silent productions to which had been added narration, music, and sound effects. As far as can be ascertained, the first original sound films to be produced specifically for classroom use were made in 1932 by ERPI; they dealt with physical science and were produced in collaboration with Dr. Robert W. Hutchins, president of the University of Chicago. As of 1943, *Film News* reported that ERPI had produced approximately forty sound films in collaboration with members of the faculty of the University of Chicago.

The American Council on Education took up the issue of educational film in the mid-1930s. On December 4 and 5, 1934, it called a preliminary conference of nationally known educators in Washington, D.C., to consider the need for an American Film Institute, "to encourage the use of the full value of the motion picture in education."[14] An American Film Institute was not to become reality until 1967; two years later it established a Center for Advanced Film Studies in Beverly Hills, California, but on the whole the Institute's involvement in film education has been lamentable and the subject of much severe criticism. The American Council on Education's plan for an American Film Institute came to nothing; but as a result of its 1937 conference on non-commercial distribution of educational films, the Rockefeller Foundation awarded a grant for the creation of the Association of School Film Libraries.

A number of American colleges and universities were finding other uses for film, uses that today might seem commonplace but were once revolutionary. In 1916, Yale established a football film library, in which it housed prints of films shot first in 28mm and later in 16mm of college games, available for study by coaches and also distributed to alumni associations. Princeton coach W. W. Roper shot football games from 1919 to 1930, and his predecessors followed the practice, with films from the late 1930s onward shot in slow motion. The University of Michigan began filming in 1937, with its swimming coach serving as staff photographer; and Elmer Leyden initiated the filming of football games at Notre Dame when he became director of athletics in 1934, not to study his own team's efforts but to review the styles of play of Notre Dame's opponents.[15]

Reid Ray photographed the 1921 football game of the University of Iowa against Indiana. Twenty-seven years later, Reid returned to Iowa to produce a ten-minute film in 35mm, *Fame of the Black and Gold*, showing university football highlights from 1921 through 1948. The film was not primarily intended for non-theatrical release, but it was distributed to theatres through the National Screen Service.

The early filming of football games by colleges and universities was an isolated example of in-house film production on campus. Film production units were not generally created until the 1940s. Film production at Indiana University was introduced in 1940, sponsored by the School of Education and the University Extension Audiovisual Center. A film unit was created at Iowa State University in 1949, primarily to produce films for the university's new television station.

That same year, Don Williams, director of the Syracuse University Audiovisual Center, was invited by the United States Information Agency to visit Iran with a view to producing educational films there. As a result of that visit, the Syracuse University Overseas Film Project was established; during its nine-year span in the 1950s, Syracuse University students filmed productions in Iran, Egypt, South Korea, Turkey, Greece, and elsewhere. According to John Mercer, "The entire overseas film operation existed under the famous 'Point 4' program of the Technical Cooperation Administration. The project progressed under a series of contracts with the U.S. Information Service and the U.S. Technical Assistance Program."[16]

Writing in *The Quarterly of Film, Radio and Television*, Flora Rheta Schreiber maintained, "The educational film, rescued from its stale, flat, and unprofitable past, is now assuming a more palatable form. Its subject matter includes everything for all grades, on all educational levels, from world geography to marriage for moderns. Producers of marked achievement, like Louis de Rochemont, include the educational film as a regular part of their output."[17]

Ms. Schreiber's comment is correct regarding Louis de Rochemont, the producer noted for the creation of the innovative newsreel series, *The March of Time*. In the 1950s, de Rochemont produced 35 educational short subjects. Ms. Schreiber might be expressing an outsider's view of the educational film field, but in every other regard her statement is incorrect. Since the 1930s, educational film had been a profitable business, as evidenced by an ever-increasing number of producers.

As of 1950, some 20,471 public high schools utilized 16mm projectors. Film was an established part of the curriculum. Yet by the 1950s, the educational film had sunk, if it had ever risen higher, to a level of mediocrity from which it was unable to recover. Educational filmmakers seemed to have little understanding of how to hold the interest of their youthful audiences. Films were dull or, worse, incomprehensible to a young mind. They were made by adults, often touted as approved by so-called experts in the educational field, but never was there input from the audiences for which they were intended. To far too many in the academic community, educational films were seen as an excuse not to teach a class rather than as an adjunct to the spoken lecture.

Admittedly there was the occasional attempt to try and relieve the gloom engendered by the presentation of an educational film. In 1957, Coronet Films, one of the largest educational producers and distributors with some 744 titles in circulation, began producing "spectaculars" for its educational audiences, on subjects such as *The French Revolution, Audubon and the Birds of America*, and *The Jamestown Colony, 1607 through 1620* (all released in 1957). Rather than spend large sums of money on production values, the hiring of props, costumes, and a large number of extras, the company tried to find pre-existing events it could utilize. For example, *The Jamestown Colony, 1607 through 1620* was filmed at the 1957 Jamestown festival. There was much truth in the company's announcement that the film "symbolizes Coronet's pioneering efforts in production on location and its working relationship with historical associations and museums to recreate history as authentically as possible."[18]

The advent of video did little to halt the activities of the educational producer and distributor. Films were simply transferred to the new medium, and it was business as usual. What ended an era in the relationship between the non-theatrical film and the classroom was computer technology. Computers offered a sophistication in teaching that neither film nor video could hope to match. They provided an interactivity between the computer screen and the user. Any talking-back to the film screen in the classroom had been argumentative rather than consultative. Further, while film held a certain amount of magic for a child, even in the classroom, in that it involved a use of machinery—the projector, whose mysteries were many—video held no such power over its viewer. The majority of American households had videotape players, and any child could and did know how to operate them. Video could offer nothing in the classroom that was not available in the home.

Similarly, videotape brought all manner of religious-oriented documentaries within easy reach of the congregation. But, ultimately, it was not video that destroyed the use of films in the churches. It was television. There is no need to rent a film or videotape of religious interest when television, particularly cable, offers such a rich, if not always varied, bounty of religious programming.

The motion picture had early in its existence turned to the Bible for inspiration: the subject was wholesome and safe, there were opportunities for a considerable amount of licentious characterization, and, above all, the stories were not protected by annoying copyright restrictions. From the 1890s onward, various companies produced versions of the *Passion Play*, which was, without question, the most filmed subject prior to 1920; and even Cecil B. DeMille's *The King of Kings* in 1927 may well be considered a more sophisticated version of the earlier offerings. Vitagraph released a three-reel version of *The Life of Moses* in 1910, and Kalem's *From the Manger to the Cross* in 1912 was one of the film industry's first feature-length productions. On the whole the religious establishment approved of the filming of Biblical subjects, even of the depiction of Christ in *From the Manger to the Cross*; and many churches would install 35mm portable projection equipment in order to screen suitable subjects for their congregations. "In all parts of the country," commented *Bohemian Magazine* in 1908, "the churches are taking advantage of this method [the motion picture] to teach their Bible lessons and to impart many religious truths, for experience has already taught them that this can be done more forcefully by the moving picture than by word of mouth."[19]

At the same time, the church was far from tolerant of the many negative aspects it saw in the fledgling film industry: the unsafe conditions within many theatre auditoriums, lurid advertising, bawdy and crude humor, and offensive subject matter. Years later, when the churches were asking the motion picture industry to make films available to them at reasonable rentals, one trade paper, *The Film Daily*, responded:

> There is no more justification for the church to expect the screen—an industry that someone else developed at tremendous cost and in the face of religious opposition all along the line—to be utilized for the advancement of their ends, however worthy, than there would be in expecting the railroads or the utilities of the country to do the same thing. When the motion picture was struggling to make something of itself, the churches were among those who booted it around from pillar to post. Now that it is somebody they are anxious to annex its influence.[20]

Providing suitable films for church use dates back at least to March 10, 1908, when the Young People's Missionary Movement, which represented all the Mission Boards of all the religious denominations in North America, gave official sanction to the use of motion pictures in education. The YMCA began handling films in 1911 and first published a classified list of film titles in 1913. In 1925 the YMCA Motion Picture Bureau was officially established, and in 1946 it was renamed Association Films. The YMCA's position as a non-theatrical film distributor was formidable; in 1939 it was reported that 127,000 reels of film were shipped from its offices in New York, Chicago (opened in 1925), and San Francisco (opened in 1938), to be viewed by some 26 million people. The subjects were varied, including scenics, government productions, and entertainment features; but they all had one thing in common, that no liquor was ever seen in any reel.

In 1916, the Federal Council of Churches of Christ in America published *Motion Pictures in Religious Education Work*, prepared by Edward M. McConoughey. A year earlier, the Methodist Episcopal Church had discussed the value of films at a New York conference; and in 1919 it embraced their use in churches. A Division of Stereopticons, Motion Pictures, and Lectures was established, which released a "white list" of approved titles and rented out films at cost. The first film made available was *The World at Columbus*, produced by D. W. Griffith, and picturing the Centenary Celebration of the Methodist Minute Men at Columbus, Ohio. The film was utilized as part of a drive to raise $120 million for the extension of Methodist work throughout the world. A second film, *The Stream of Life* (1919), was an inspirational drama directed by Horace G. Plimpton, which was screened not only in churches but also at a New York theatre rented by the Methodist Church.

The Knights of Columbus used motion pictures as part of their "Americanization" program. Supreme Secretary William J. McGinley explained in 1920: "We have found a most encouraging demand among alien-born ex-service men for literature in connection with patriotic and historic pictures they have witnessed. They will absorb what is known as America—the atmosphere and traditions of our country—quite willingly when offered them as an incidental matter to practical technical training; while they resent uplift methods of Americanization."[21]

At least three religious film companies were organized in New York in 1914: the Religious Pictures Corporation, the Sacred and Historic Film Company, and the Catholic Film Association. As its name implies, the last was founded "to buy and distribute educational and amusement pictures to Catholic churches." It should be emphasized that films for churches were not limited to religious tableaux. For example, the Monarch Film Company, active from 1915 into the early 1920s, offered "sermonettes" on subjects such as prayer, God, and worship, while another company from the same period, the New Era Film Company, distributed films of sacred songs with the action on screen timed to synchronize with the church organist's playing of the same melodies.

Motion picture brought the people into churches, entertained and/or enlightened them (hopefully both), and further proved a much-needed source of income. "Pictures in the pulpit mean more people in the pews" was the rallying cry of many church officials.[22] As early as 1913, the Church of St. Jude and the Nativity in Philadelphia was charging a one-penny admission to weekly film screenings, with local Boy Scouts serving as ushers. Writing in *Moving Pictures in the Church*, published in 1921, Pastor Roy L. Smith commented, "We find that pictures can be made to serve three purposes in the general program of the church. 1. In the services of worship. 2. For social entertainment. 3. In the educational program."[23]

In converting their facilities into theatres, churches could also turn a fair profit. The average cost of renting a program of films in 1921 was between $10.00 and $12.50. The audience could number between 400 and 650, and the collection amounted to between $8.00 and $20.00. Popular films could be rented by church groups after their initial release at a fraction of the rental fees charged to theatres. The Garrick Theatre, Minneapolis, rented the 1919 William Fox production, *Evangeline*, for $5,000 for a one-week first run. A year later, a church in the same city could rent the film for $25.00 for a one-day screening.

Pastor Smith argued, "Let the church go into the entertainment business for the sake of the service it can render and be satisfied when the actual cost of the service is met by the income."[24] But many congregations used motion pictures for fund-raising purposes. Further, a popular film shown in a Sunday school class could often draw children away from the Sunday schools of other denominations. The Reverend G. H. Ashworth of Sycamore, Illinois, noted a 500 percent increase in attendance when he introduced films to his church. The Reverend W. G. Godsell of the Westfield, Illinois, Congregational Church delighted his Sunday school children with the choice of subject matter at weekly screenings, but he was forced to resign when the congregation complained that the films taught the boys to "emulate cowboys."[25]

Motion pictures were becoming big business to church groups, which was angering legitimate film exhibitors. The trade paper *The Exhibitors' Herald* complained that rather than "wresting another weapon from the devil and converting it to its own purpose," the use of films by churches "has progressed to the point where it may be regarded as a commercial menace by those who look to the business of exhibiting pictures for a livelihood. . . . Entertainment certainly is no part of the proper business of churches. They are entitled to fullest cooperation in functions that come within the sphere of their legitimate work—and fullest opposition in this foreign endeavor."[26]

Perhaps because the film industry was unwilling to take on such a powerful adversary as organized religion, whose tacit approval it was always to need, there was no abatement in the use of entertainment films in churches. Nor was there any major attempt by the various denominations to organize their film-related activities, apart from the National Legion of Decency, formed in 1934 by the Catholic Bishops of the United States not to produce or distribute films but to rate them on moral grounds.

In 1941, the American Baptist Convention established a Department of Visual Aids, "to produce motion pictures on our Baptist mission fields around the world." It produced its first sound film, *Out of the Dust*, shot on 16mm, in 1945; and by 1956 was operating three film libraries—in New York, Chicago, and Berkeley—with 600 motion pictures and filmstrips in release. The Protestant Film Commission was organized in 1945 to produce 16mm religious films. Its most important achievement was a 45-minute feature titled *A Wonderful Life*, starring Hollywood actor James Dunn as a small-town businessman who worked quietly for the betterment of his local church; only at his death did his family and friends realize that his was "a wonderful life." As of 1952, the film had been shown in 22,000 churches.

On March 25, 1942, the Religious Film Association was organized in New York by sixteen leading Protestant church agencies and with financial assistance from the Harmon Foundation, to help congregations use visual aids to their best advantage. In 1952, the Association released the first films from the Broadcasting and Film Commission of the National Council of Churches. *We Hold These Truths: "Are Slums and Segregation the Sole Heritage of My People?"* was the story of a Korean War-bound black soldier on leave in Washington, D.C. *Challenge to Africa* dealt with the struggle between Christianity and Communism on the African continent.

The Harmon Foundation had been active in the religious film field since 1925. In 1938, it created the African Motion Picture Project, which, as of 1948, had produced eight 16mm silent films on the work of missionaries in Africa designed for church use "to let the people at home get a glimpse of life in the mission fields."[27]

The United Presbyterian Church of North America had first become involved with motion pictures in 1925, producing a 35mm short subject on missionary work in Egypt. Two decades later, in 1947, it established an Audio-Visual Office in Pittsburgh, headed by the Reverend Orville L. Kuhn.

As is obvious, the 1940s was very much a decade of expansion by religious organizations into motion picture production and distribution. In February 1946, *The Educational Screen* began publication of a monthly column "The Church Department," edited by William S. Hockman. One incentive for the revival of interest in films by American churches may have been the 1939 founding of Cathedral Films by the Reverend James K. Friedrich. Based in Hollywood, the company's first production was the feature-length *The Great Commandment*, which was released in 16mm by Films Incorporated and purchased for theatrical release by 20th Century-Fox for $170,000.

Religion and education were combined in the activities of Bob Jones University, located in Greenville, South Carolina. Under the direction of Katherine Stenholm, the Division of Cinema was created at the fundamentalist religious university in 1950. The university's production unit was named Unusual Films and utilized virtually all university departments in its work. All productions were religious in content, and the trademark of Unusual Films was an angel carrying a camera in its arms.

Dr. Bob Jones, Jr., president of the university since its renaming from Bob Jones College in 1947, pointed out, "An angel is a messenger and our films are films with a message."[28]

The first two productions of Unusual Films, released in 1951, were *Light of the World*, an "illustrated sermon" based on a popular message frequently preached by Bob Jones, Sr., and a feature-length production, shot in color, of Shakespeare's *Macbeth*.

A number of illustrative sermon films were produced in the early years, but it quickly became apparent that the university's background in classical theatre made Unusual Films best suited to the production of dramatic films. *Wine of Morning*, released in 1954 and based on the life of Barabbas, was a two-hour drama that became immediately successful within the conservative Christian community and set the tone for future productions. It also led to the university's offering Bachelor of Science and Master of Arts degrees in film production. Unusual Films and Dr. Stenholm were founding members of the University Film Producers Association (now the University Film and Video Association); through the efforts of that organization, *Wine of Morning* was selected to represent the United States at a special university division of the 1958 Cannes Film Festival.

Later Unusual Films productions include *Red Runs the River* (1963), *Flame in the Wind* (1971), *Sheffey* (1978), *Beyond the Night* (1983), and *The Printing* (1990). The large-scale nature of these productions is primarily due to the support services provided by Bob Jones University, including the participation of students and faculty as performers, catering by the University Dining Common, and recording by the University Orchestra of scores provided by the music faculty. With the exception of laboratory work, every aspect of production, from script to screen, is handled in-house, with the films intended as a ministry rather than for profit.

America's best regarded evangelist Billy Graham was a student at Bob Jones College for four months in 1936–1937; he left because he was more interested in baseball than in the school's academic teachings. In 1951, Graham founded Billy Graham Evangelistic Films, Inc., which produced documentaries of Graham's crusades and fictional evangelical subjects under the direction of Richard Ross. The company name was changed to World Wide Pictures in 1957, at which time it was merged with Ross' Great Commission Film Company.

NOTES

1. Orrin G. Cocks, "Libraries and Motion Pictures—An Ignored Educational Agency," *Library Journal*, vol. XIX, no. 9 (September 1914), p. 666.

2. Ibid., p. 668.

3. Melvil Dewey, "Our Next Half Century," *Library Journal*, vol. LI, no. 18 (October 15, 1926), p. 889.

4. Gerald Doan McDonald, *Educational Motion Pictures and Libraries* (Chicago: American Library Association, 1942), p. vi.

5. Ibid., p. vii.

6. The last issue was vol. XVII, nos. 2, 3, and 4.

7. For more information, see F. Dean McClusky, "A-V 1905–1955," *Educational Screen*, vol. XXXIV, no. 4 (April 1955), pp. 160–62, and Jane McCammon, "St. Louis: A-V Pioneer," *ibid.*, pp. 163–65.

8. Reverend W. H. Jackson, "The Moving Picture as an Educator," *Moving Picture Annual and Yearbook for 1912* (New York: The Moving Picture World, 1913), p. 30.

9. "Editorial," *Educational Screen*, vol. I, no. 1 (January 1922), p. 5.

10. In 1970 DAVI became part of the Association for Educational Communications and Technology (AECT), 1126 16th Street, N.W., Washington, D.C., 20036.

11. "Editorial," *Educational Screen*, vol. VII, no. 1 (March 1928), p. 5.

12. Terry Ramsaye, "The Picture and Education," *Educational Screen*, vol. IX, no. 6 (May 1930), p. 136.

13. Quoted in *Educational Screen*, vol. VIII, no. 10 (December 1929), p. 295.

14. *Educational Screen*, vol. XIV, no. 3 (March 1935), p. 72; see also Edgar Dale, "A Discussion Concerning the Proposed American Film Institute," *Educational Screen*, vol. XIV, no. 9 (November 1935), pp. 249–52.

15. For more information, see "To Whom Films Have Done the Most," *Film News*, vol. I, no. 12 (December 1940), pp. 1, 7.

16. John Mercer, *The Informational Film* (Champaign, Ill.: Stipes Publishing Company, 1981), p. 42.

17. Flora Rheta Schreiber, "New York—A Cinema Capital," *Quarterly of Film, Radio and Television*, vol. VII, no. 3 (Spring 1953), p. 269.

18. *Educational Screen & Audio-Visual Guide*, vol. XXXVI, no. 11 (December 1957), p. 577.

19. John R. Meader, "The Story of the Picture That Moves," *Bohemian Magazine*, September 1908, p. 363.

20. Quoted in *Educational Screen*, vol. X, no. 7 (September 1931), pp. 206–7.

21. Quoted in "The Motion-Picture as a 'Handmaid of Religion,' " *Literary Digest*, vol. LXV, no. 7 (May 15, 1920), p. 46.

22. Ibid.

23. Roy L. Smith, *Moving Pictures in the Church* (New York: Abingdon Press, 1921), p. 17. Smith was the pastor of Simpson Methodist Church, Minneapolis, and a contributing editor to *The Moving Picture Age*.

24. *Ibid.*, p. 41.

25. Reported in William F. Kruse, " . . . Not Born Yesterday," *Educational Screen & Audio-Visual Guide*, vol. XXXVIII, no. 2 (February 1959), pp. 77–78.

26. Quoted in "The Motion-Picture as a 'Handmaid of Religion,' " *Literary Digest*, vol. LXV, no. 7 (May 15, 1920), p. 47.

27. *Educational Screen*, vol. XXIV, no. 5 (May 1948), p. 193.

28. Quoted in " 'Angel with a Camera in His Arms' Brings Bob Jones' Films to World Audience," *Business Screen*, vol. XXII, no. 2 (April 28, 1961), p. 42.

SIX

The Chronicles of America

One series of films is superior to any other production in the non-theatrical subgenres of business, educational, or religious subjects, "The Chronicles of America." It was the most ambitious non-theatrical production ever attempted, combining "Hollywood" techniques with the highest of educational standards. The series proved that it was possible to introduce quality filmmaking and high production values to educational films—that "educational" was not a synonym for boring or cheaply made. To a large extent, the Chronicles of America series was evidence that the non-theatrical film could be in every way as appealing to an audience and as praiseworthy to the critics as any theatrical feature.

The similarity between the Chronicles of America and a theatrical feature of the day comes from the fact that the former utilized many film industry craftsmen in its production. The major difference was that no Hollywood production was of the scope or size of the Chronicles of America. At a time when a typical Hollywood feature was produced in a matter of weeks, the Chronicles of America took months. While the average Hollywood feature was six reels in length, the Chronicles of America was to be released in one hundred reels.

In many respects, the Chronicles of America is comparable to D. W. Griffith's 1915 production of *The Birth of a Nation*. It lacks the artistry and the controversial subject matter of the Griffith epic, but it possessed the same sincerity, a similar scope and vision in its attempt to chronicle

American history; and it was a pioneer in the production of non-
theatrical films just as *The Birth of a Nation* was the production that
established the motion picture as an art form and proved that the feature-
length film was a viable and acceptable reality.

The series had its origins in the fifty-volume *The Chronicles of America*
published by the Yale University Press. George Parmly Day, the president of the press and its founder in 1908, explained:

> This series is designed to present the entire story of America, so that it
> may be read even by those whose time for books is very limited and who
> are not in the habit of reading history. Each of the fifty narratives is a
> topical unit and may be read separately, but all are so related that they
> form one continuous and complete story. These narratives are written by
> competent authors, and in them the traditions of the nation are made real
> and vivid.
>
> More than five years was consumed in the preparation of *The Chronicles
> of America*. The work was definitely begun in March, 1916. Ten volumes
> of the fifty were published in August, 1918, ten more in February, 1919,
> ten more in July, 1919, five in December, 1919, five in March, 1920, and
> ten in August, 1921, completing the series.
>
> Meanwhile three editions of the whole series were practically absorbed
> by the public before the work could be completed. A fourth edition, con-
> sisting of 10,000 sets of the fifty volumes, has since been printed. Already
> thousands of American citizens, many of whom, perhaps, never thought
> of reading history before, are reading these books for recreation.[1]

The initial idea to film the books came apparently not from the Yale
University Press, but from the publishing house of Glasgow & Brook,
which was handling the physical publication of the series on behalf of
the Yale University Press. The books were sold on a subscription basis;
and even with only ten printed, pledged subscriptions amounted to
more than $2.25 million. Many of the subscribers commented that the
books could be adapted into a superior motion picture series, and the
idea intrigued Robert Glasgow, the head of Glasgow & Brook. Professor
Richard Webster of Columbia University mentioned to Glasgow that one
of the university's visiting professors of journalism, Robert E. Mac-
Alarney, the former city editor of the *New York Tribune*, was managing
editor at Famous Players-Lasky, the production wing of Paramount Pictures. A meeting was arranged among Glasgow, MacAlarney, and H.
Whitman Bennett, production manager with Famous Players-Lasky. The
meeting took place in New York at the Harvard Club. It is perhaps most
remarkable that at this stage of the discussions the one university not
involved was Yale!

Early in 1920, Glasgow and MacAlarney decided to go ahead and hire
a scenario editor named Arthur Edwin Krows to study the books and

report on the possibility of their being filmed. Krows was a relatively unimportant figure in the film industry; he had written the scenarios for a couple of Vitagraph productions, *The Winchester Woman* (1919) and *The Birth of a Soul* (1920); and if he is to be accorded a footnote in the history of the cinema it will be as author of the series on the history of the non-theatrical film, "Motion Pictures—Not for Theatres," in *The Educational Screen*. In addition to hiring Krows, Glasgow and MacAlarney approached Paramount as to the cost of the studio's producing five eight-reel features based on *The Chronicles of America*, covering the years from Columbus to Woodrow Wilson. The initial idea was to utilize funds on a revolving basis, with the profits from the first feature going towards the production of the second, with an opening investment of only $20,000. Paramount provided a verbal estimate of one million dollars. It was obvious that the project was too large for Glasgow and Mac-Alarney to tackle without support from Yale University.

Further, Glasgow decided that the film series should be not strictly dramatizations of the books, but rather a series of separate works to be prepared by screenwriters who would receive proper credit for their work. Krows wrote the first two scenarios, for *Columbus* and *Jamestown*, taking into account the need to document his sources. As he recalled later:

> The scripts certainly were unique in form, made so to accommodate the peculiar demands of the situation. They were typed on long, foolscap sheets to care for elaborate footnotes on each page, which gave historical justification and amplification of every major point. In the first two scripts alone, the supporting notes totalled more than 50,000 words. Information as to physical appearances, including costumes; how houses and fortifications were constructed; ages, heights, weights and mannerisms of the respective characters; full descriptions of properties—all were to be found there, convenient to the hand of any and every person who might have to do with editorial supervision or production. There was even talk of printing these scenarios for the guidance of teachers who might use the completed pictures in class.[2]

On June 6, 1921, on what Krows remembered as a lovely summer's morning, he and Robert Glasgow presented the two scenarios in the Yale University board room to a group that included George Parmly Day and Allen Johnson, chairman of the university's Department of History and general editor of the *Chronicles of America*. The representatives of the university were impressed, and the scenarios were forwarded to the Council's Committee on Publications, which endorsed the project on September 26, 1921.

The Council's committee adopted the following resolution:

Voted, to approve in general the proposal for the production by the Yale University Press or under its auspices of a series of motion pictures based on The Chronicles of America provided the work is carried on under the following conditions and under such further regulations as the committee may deem wise:

(1) An editor shall be appointed by the council's committee on publications, and no "continuities" shall be accepted until these have been studied and revised by experts engaged by the editor and until the editor has certified to the committee that the said "continuities" meet his approval.

(2) The director to be appointed for the production of the proposed motion pictures shall be approved by the council's committee on publications and no picture shall be released until the finished product shall have been seen and approved for release by the council's committee on publications on the basis of their own judgment or on the basis of reports made to them by such expert advisors as they may designate.

An editorial board of three was appointed, consisting of Dr. Frank E. Spaulding, Sterling Professor of School Administration and Head of the Department of Education at Yale; Professor Nathaniel Wright Stephenson, formerly of the Department of History in the College of Charleston and later an exchange professor at Yale; and Dr. Max Farrand, professor of American history at Yale. They consulted with an additional group representing some of the best-known names in the study of American history: Allen Johnson, Charles M. Andrews, and DeForest Van Slyck at Yale; John Spencer Bassett of Smith College, the secretary of the American Historical Society; Clarence G. Alvord of the University of Minnesota; St. George L. Sioussat of the University of Pennsylvania; Yates Snowden of the University of South Carolina; Carl Becker of Cornell University; Dixon Ryan Fox of Columbia University; Irving B. Richman; Colonel William Wood; David I. Bushnell, Jr.; Matthew Page Andrews; Wilfrid Jordon, curator of Independence Hall, Philadelphia; Lyon G. Tyler and William G. Stannard of the Virginia Historical Society; Otto Rothert and R. T. Ballard Thurston of the Filson Club, Louisville; Worthington C. Ford of the Massachusetts Historical Society; James P. Monroe and Edwin B. Worthen of the Lexington Historical Society; Allen French of the Concord Historical Society; Joseph Shafer, Superintendent of the State Historical Society, Madison, Wisconsin; Eugene C. Barker of the University of Texas; Archer M. Huntington, President of the Hispanic Museum; and Professor George Pierce Baker of Harvard University.

Historical costumes were subject to approval by Harry A. Ogden, and sets were approved by Professor Fiske Kimball of New York University, a noted authority on architectural development in the United States.

"Detailed accuracy in accessories and costumes, in all properties, is not only desirable but essential," explained Robert E. MacAlarney.[3]

"There will be no George Washington chopping down the cherry-tree and (hush) Captain John Smith will not be quite the hero he tried to make himself out to be," commented Joe Toye in the *Boston Herald*. "Remember that famous painting of Washington Crossing the Delaware? Well, first of all, the crossing was made at night; second, that boat couldn't hold all the men that are in it, and, third, none but a fool, and George was far from that, would stand as George is shown in the painting. 'The truth, the whole truth and nothing but the truth, so help me, Hadley,' is the motto of those back of the enterprise."[4]

At the same time, MacAlarney was quick to point out that "Our historians will interfere in no way with the technical side of production. They will attend strictly to the historical accuracy of it all. . . . These pictures will be as perfect technically as the accumulative knowledge of the motion picture industry can make them. The lighting will be the best, the actors chosen for their dramatic ability. History is dramatic, but it will not be overdone. There is no need of that."[5]

While the academic community was gathering to vet the scenarios, events were moving ahead on the production side. Robert MacAlarney was appointed business manager, and Arthur Edwin Krows was allowed to appoint a staff of four, consisting of two researchers, a secretary and "a girl to do routine copying."[6] Carlyle Ellis was appointed production manager, and he hired Thomas H. Swinton as assistant director and Walter T. Pritchard as cameraman. Production space was rented in the Guaranty Building at Fifth Avenue and Forty-fourth Street, New York. In January 1922, the incorporation of the Chronicles of America Picture Corporation was announced, with George Parmly Day as its president, Robert Glasgow as vice president, Arthur Edwin Krows as secretary, and Arthur Brook treasurer.

Yale alumni purchased stock in the new corporation, the project received warm approval from the educational community, and four scenarios had been approved by the Council's committee. On April 5, 1922, Robert Glasgow gave a talk at the Kiwanis Club in New York on the friendly relationship between the United States and his native Canada. He returned to his office and died at his desk. MacAlarney eulogized his colleague: "Mr. Glasgow was a Canadian, it is true, but if ever a man typified America in every fibre in him it was Robert Glasgow. What is more, he believed deeply and firmly in America and what our country stands for."[7] Thereafter Robert Glasgow was totally forgotten as the originator of the film project. His name did not appear in any later publicity, and MacAlarney took over Glasgow's duties.

At that time, the production plan was to film one hundred reels, with separate short subjects covering the various eras in American history. The original breakdown was:

> Seven films in twenty-one reels on "The Morning of America," covering the English pioneers in the New World, the struggle for possession, and the expulsion of the French.
>
> Three films in nine reels on "The Winning of Independence," covering the New World's refusal to submit to dictation from the English King and Parliament and the battlefields of the Revolution, following Washington.
>
> Two films in six reels on "The Young Republic," covering the new government, the Constitution, Hamilton, and Jefferson.
>
> Eight films in twenty-four reels on "The Vision of the West," covering the conquest of the continent from the Alleghenies to the Pacific Ocean.
>
> Five films in fifteen reels on "The Storm of Secession," covering the preservation of the Union, the extermination of slavery, battlefields of the Civil War, Stonewall Jackson, Lee, and Grant.
>
> Five films in twenty-five reels on "The Age of Power," covering the influx of immigrants, the mechanical revolution, and America in the twentieth century.

A few months later the number of films and the overall subjects were revised to nine films in twenty-two reels on "The Morning of America," seven films in sixteen reels on "The Winning of Independence," six films in sixteen reels on "The Young Republic," eight films in twenty-two reels on "The Vision of the West," six films in eighteen reels on "The Civil War," and five films in twenty-five reels on "The Age of Power."

The first film in the series to go into production was *Columbus*, in the summer of 1922. Carlyle Ellis had assumed that he would be director, but he was replaced by a minor theatrical director, Edwin L. Hollywood, who had been active in the film industry as a director or assistant director since 1914. Frank Heath was named Hollywood's assistant. Interior scenes were filmed at the Vitagraph Studios in the Flatbush area of Brooklyn. (Although it is not possible to document the link, Vitagraph appears to have had more than a passing interest in the project, through not only the use of its studio space but also the members of its scenario department, including Krows and his successor William Basil Courtney.) The city of Chicago agreed to the use of the reproductions of the ships of Columbus moored in its Jackson Park lagoon; and although the Nina and the Pinta could not be moved, the Santa Maria was considered sufficiently seaworthy and towed out to Lake Michigan for a number of crucial shots. The first scene to be filmed showed the messenger sent by Queen Isabella to overtake Columbus and the sailor's wife waving goodbye to the Santa Maria. This was filmed near Montauk, Long Island, which Yale academics agreed resembled Spanish topography. Additional exterior scenes were shot at Mount Kisco (standing in for the garden at the palace of King John of Portugal) and Huntington, Long Island (for the La Rábida Monastery).

A well-known Broadway actor with no previous screen experience, Fred Eric, who made only one other film later in 1923, was cast in the title role. Playing opposite him was a minor opera singer and film actress, Dolores Cassinelli, who had been appearing on screen for some years. Others in the cast were Paul McAllister (John II of Portugal), Howard Truesdell (Bishop of Ceuta), Leslie Stowe (Juan Pérez), and Robert Gaillard (King Ferdinand).

Edwin L. Hollywood shot 52,000 feet of film, which he edited down to a rough cut of 8,500 feet. A further 3,500 feet was cut, leaving a completed feature film of approximately 60 minutes' running time. Immediately following completion of *Columbus*, Edwin L. Hollywood began direction of the second film in the series, *Jamestown*, set in 1612; it dealt with the isolation of the Virginia community by both the Indians and the Spanish, the taking hostage of Pocahontas, and her subsequent marriage to John Rolfe. In order to conserve costs, the entire film was shot at the former Kinemacolor Studio at Whitestone, Long Island, where a replica of the Jamestown settlement was built. The production was not without its grim side, when an extra playing a seminaked Indian developed pneumonia and died.

The cast was pretty much the same as for *Columbus*. Dolores Cassinelli starred again, this time as Pocahontas, supported by Robert Gaillard (as Sir Thomas Dale), Harry Kendall (George Yeardley), Leslie Stowe (Reverend Richard Buck), Paul McAllister (Don Dieo de Molina), and Leslie Austin (John Rolfe).

Both films were very well received by both the popular and the academic press. *Photoplay* (December 1923) pointed out that *Columbus* was "for the grown-ups, too," adding, "This is the greatest stride yet taken to develop the educational value of the motion picture, and the originators of the idea believe it will do much to promote good and intelligent citizenship." Writing in *The World's Work* (September 1924), Clayton Hamilton opined that the two features were "much more interesting and entertaining than the majority of motion pictures that are concocted deliberately for the amusement of the multitude."

Hamilton's opinion was one with which more and more individuals involved in the project concurred. It was, therefore, not totally surprising when George Parmly Day announced in the fall of 1923 that the Chronicles of America series would be distributed to theatres by Pathé Exchange, Inc., which would also handle the physical aspects of nontheatrical distribution on behalf of the Yale University Press Film Service. Day explained:

While the producers have never lost sight of their primary purpose in the preparation of these motion pictures, to provide a new and effective apparatus to aid in the teaching of history, they have always remembered that if "The Chronicles of America in Photoplays" could be beautifully conceived, they would appeal to the theatergoing public no less strongly than to teachers and students, because of the dramatic quality inherent in the story of our country from its discovery to Appomattox.

The release of "The Chronicles of America Photoplays" through the theaters marks the dawn of a new day for motion pictures, for if the motion pictures shown in its theaters as well as in its schools are of a high standard of excellence no community need fear for the influence undoubtedly and most effectively exercised by "the movies."[8]

It was a skillful move on Day's part to suggest his series might allay fears felt by many Americans regarding the motion picture. Theatrical producers and distributors were thus seduced away from any objections they might wish to raise as to a university's becoming involved in commercial aspects of film production and distribution, and exhibitors were enticed into booking the films for the betterment of the community and their own place within it. From the outset, it was very obvious that the Chronicles of America were as much about patriotism and good citizenship as about American history. When first announcing the film series, Day had said:

It is the hope of the organizers that the pictures will prove to be more than a profitable business enterprise—that they prove of real value in the development of patriotism and good citizenship.

Of course good citizenship means intelligent citizenship. In order to know where we are now and where we are going, we must know where we have come from and what has happened to us on the way. History is experience handed down. A physician must have the history of his case before he can diagnose it intelligently. A lawyer must be thoroughly grounded in the precedents which make up the law in any case he is handling. In the same way a citizen, to be a good citizen, must know the experience of his nation in order that he may form intelligent opinions. The galvanic power of the screen, its power to arouse and stimulate the faculties, whether rightly or wrongly used, has never been disputed. It is now proposed to apply this power to American history, studied hitherto through the medium of the written word alone.[9]

With the completion of *Jamestown*, Edwin L. Hollywood left the series, and, for reasons unknown, never made another film, although he lived for a further thirty-five years. Arthur Edwin Krows also left the project. "I began to break under the strain," he recalled. "I was persuaded to take the accumulated time of an unused month's vacation; but I returned in a state of even greater distress and realized that I must withdraw for my own good. Accordingly, though with a heavy hand, I bought my way out of my contract."[10] Krows' departure from the project may in part have been out of a lack of understanding on his part as to the academic requirements of the series. He had hired a group of news-papermen and film trade paper writers to submit scenarios for later productions. None of those scenarios was ever used, if they were even completed, and it is obvious they would not have met the academic standards of the Council's Committee at Yale.

Production on the series was falling behind schedule, in large part because the academic community is not used to producing anything to a deadline, with the possible exception of degrees for its students. The series was budgeted at $12.50 per foot of released film, but it was im-possible to keep within that budget when production deadlines could not be met. Arthur Edwin Krows wrote:

> Stories, true or not, were rife about the Chronicles casting director hav-ing to submit all principals chosen to the scrutiny of professors untrained in such delicate work; about a company and production crew being held on full salary in an Adirondack location for upwards of eleven weeks while alleged experts debated whether the cabin occupied by the characters should have its logs notched or mortised at the corners; about a professor who allegedly scrapped a set at shooting time because a decorative molding was out of period; about some regimental buttons which were never to be seen closer than about twenty feet, having to be remolded for an entire company of soldiers who were on salary in the interval. And, even as rumors such as these will do, they inspired a disrespect, a tongue-in-cheek service from most of those who were engaged to give a hand. The word spread like wild-fire through the theatrical district that here was a fine, fat, foolish cow waiting to be milked, and players and technical men flocked without conscience to share the cream.[11]

In reality, production of the Chronicles of America series had begun to take on the characteristics of many Hollywood productions. The pri-mary difference was that the time-wasting temperament was provided not by the actors but by the professorial advisors, whose money-wasting reads remarkably like the worst excesses of director Erich von Stroheim.

In an effort to speed production, Robert MacAlarney decided to con-tract with an outside production company in the form of the Film Guild. A New York–based production company with high ideals, the Film Guild was established in 1923 by Townsend Martin from Princeton; Yale grad-uates Frank Tuttle, James Ashmore Creelman, and Dwight Deere Wi-man; and Fred Waller, Jr., who did not graduate from high school. Tuttle was to become a prominent Hollywood director in the 1930s and 1940s, later blacklisted for his leftist leanings. Fred Waller, Jr., later invented the three-projector wide-screen system Cinerama, first seen at the 1939

New York World's Fair and commercially exploited in the 1950s. The Film Guild produced four features, *Second Fiddle* (1923), *Puritan Passions* (1923), *Youthful Cheaters* (1923), and *Grit* (1924), all starring Glenn Hunter.

The Film Guild's Yale connection may, in part, have persuaded the Council's committee to go along with MacAlarney. From a financial standpoint it was a sensible move in that the Film Guild was apparently able to use some of the sets and costumes from *Puritan Passions* in its Chronicles of America productions, of which there were at least two, *Peter Stuyvesant* (1924) and *The Puritans* (1924). As Laura Kay Palmer has noted in her 1991 study of the careers of Osgood and Anthony Perkins,[12] the two films were some of the first to feature the talented Osgood Perkins. At the time, he was not a "name" actor, but from a modern viewpoint he is the only known player in the cast.

The original proposal in 1922 had been to produce thirty-five separate films. In reality only fifteen were made, perhaps in part because eventually even MacAlarney and Krows' successor William Basil Courtney grew tired of dealing with the Yale bureaucracy, particularly when several members of the advisory committee decided to write the scenarios themselves. The following is a complete listing of the films in the series, produced between 1923 and 1925:

> *Columbus* (five reels), adapted from *The Spanish Conquerors* by Irving Berdine Richman.
>
> *Jamestown* (five reels), adapted from *Pioneers of the Old South* by Mary Johnston.
>
> *The Pilgrims* (three reels), adapted from *The Fathers of New England* by Charles M. Andrews.
>
> *The Puritans* (three reels), adapted from *The Fathers of New England* by Charles M. Andrews, with a screenplay by the author's wife, Mrs. Evangeline W. Andrews.
>
> *Peter Stuyvesant* (three reels), adapted from *Dutch and English on the Hudson* by Maud Wilder Goodwin, with a screenplay by Professor Dixon Ryan Fox of Columbia University and William Basil Courtney.
>
> *The Gateway to the West* (three reels), adapted from *The Conquest of New France* by George M. Wrong. The film marked the first appearance in the series of George Washington, as a young colonel sent by Governor Robert Dinwiddie of Virginia to lodge a protest with the French. A production unit, under the direction of Professor Nathaniel W. Stephenson, spent six weeks on location in three states along the Appalachian range.
>
> *Wolfe and Montcalm* (three reels), adapted from *The Conquest of New France* by George M. Wrong, with a screenplay by Kenneth Webb.
>
> *The Evening of the Revolution* (three reels), adapted from a Chronicle of the same name by Carl Becker, with a screenplay by Professor George Pierce Baker of Harvard University.

The Declaration of Independence (three reels), adapted from *The Eve of the Revolution* by Carl Becker, with a screenplay by William Basil Courtney.

Yorktown (three reels), adapted from *Washington and His Comrades in Arms* by George M. Wrong, with a screenplay by Professor Nathaniel Wright Stephenson.

Vincennes (three reels), adapted from *The Old Northwest* by Frederic Austin Ogg.

Daniel Boone (three reels), adapted from *Pioneers of the Old Southwest* by Constance Lindsay Skinner, with a screenplay by Esther W. Bates, a student of the "47 Workshop" at Harvard University and an instructor in dramatics at Boston University.

The Frontier Women (three reels), adapted from *Pioneers of the Old Southwest* by Constance Lindsay Skinner, with a screenplay by Professor Nathaniel Wright Stephenson.

Alexander Hamilton (three reels), adapted from *Washington and His Colleagues* by Henry Jones Ford, with a screenplay by Professor Allen Johnson. The film was shot in part at Morristown, New Jersey, with the approval of the Daughters of the American Revolution.

Dixie (three reels), adapted from *The Day of the Confederacy* by Nathaniel W. Stephenson, with a screenplay by his wife, Mrs. Martha Tucker Stephenson.

The entire series was as well received as the first episodes. *The Educational Screen* editorialized that the Chronicles of America were "historical films produced by men who know history and the meaning of history." The film trade paper *The Moving Picture World* hailed the series as "one of the greatest innovations in the history of the motion picture industry," continuing,

In The Chronicles of America series there is found a perfect blending. History, authentic and without distortion, is visualized; but here are also found the film technician and the dramatic artist to assure that the production requisites of photography, direction, and acting are skillfully carried out. Authenticity and accuracy in history are sought for, but the matter of entertaining action and situations are carefully attended to, and every dramatic value naturally embodied in the stories is accorded the fullest and most skillful expression that practical experience in the art of screen entertainment can give it.

Each of The Chronicles of America is an epic in the complete picturization of the dramatic high lights of America's past. To designate them as dramatic and thrilling is but to attribute to them the qualities inherent in all truly entertaining pictures. While the Chronicles possess these essential points of merit their appeal is far deeper, far dearer to the heart of the American people. Their keynote is patriotism. They are pure American pictures depicting the struggles, sacrifices, adventures, conflicts, and accomplishments of our forefathers. They represent an entertaining, picturesque, and authentic presentation of the birth and development of America. Their authenticity is a notable asset since the events portrayed are so gripping in themselves, their dramatic effect so powerful and the qualities of courage, faith, and patriotism so humanly revealed that the narrative becomes an engrossing story.[13]

Comments such as this, coupled with the early commercial success of the Chronicles of America series, may well have influenced the production of two major feature films dealing with the revolutionary wars and both released in 1924: D. W. Griffith's *America* and the Marion Davies vehicle *Janice Meredith*.

Films in the Chronicles of America series have been preserved at both the Museum of Modern Art and the Library of Congress. From today's viewpoint, they appear slow moving, lacking in dramatic development, and basically dull. In the 1930s, a distributor commented, "We are, of course, the first to recognize that their [the series] entertainment value is low—actually has been since the beginning, when action was purposely held to a minimum."[14] Yet the influence of these films on the commercial film industry was considerable. Above all, the Chronicles of America proved there was an audience for historical dramas and costume pictures, genres producers had dismissed as not commercial. In the 1920s, the American film industry produced three features each on the revolutionary wars and the colonial period in American history, plus twenty-one feature-length films on the Civil War, ranging from the serious *Abraham Lincoln* (1924) to the comic *Hands Up!* (1926) and *The General* (1927).

Meeting some surprising resistance to the use of the films in classrooms, the Yale Department of Education began a series of studies under the guidance of Professor Irving N. Countryman. The results were published by the Yale University Press as *Motion Pictures in History Teaching* by Daniel V. Knowlton and J. Warren Tilton. The American Museum of Natural History purchased three complete 35mm sets, the New York Public Schools System acquired nine 16mm sets, and the Chicago Board of Education purchased fourteen.

The Chronicles of America was released in a 16mm version in 1930. Suggestions that sound be added to the series were generally ignored, with one authority suggesting that "sound would lessen their authenticity."[15] The desperate need for early television programming led to the complete series being aired on the NBC station WNBT beginning December 1945. (Presumably there must have been some musical accompaniment, just as the series was screened in commercial theatres with live music from a piano, organ, or orchestra.) The Chronicles of America last gained attention in the educational community in the fall of 1959, when the Yale University Press Film Service released the entire series in filmstrip form under its original title. In that the visual education movement had begun with magic lantern slides showing a series of still images, the new release meant that the Chronicles of America series had come full circle in a period of thirty-five years.

NOTES

1. Quoted in "Yale's Movie Version of American History," *Literary Digest,* vol. LXXII, no. 9 (March 4, 1922), pp. 41–42.

2. Arthur Edwin Krows, "Motion Pictures—Not for Theatres," *Educational Screen,* vol. XXI, no. 3 (March 1942), p. 104.

3. *School and Society,* vol. XVI, no. 398 (August 12, 1922), p. 183.

4. Quoted in "Yale's Movie Version of American History," *Literary Digest,* vol. LXXII, no. 9 (March 4, 1922), p. 41.

5. Ibid.

6. Arthur Edwin Krows, "Motion Pictures—Not for Theatres," *Educational Screen,* vol. XXI, no. 3 (March 1942), p. 105.

7. Quoted in Hawthorne Daniel, "American History in Moving Pictures," *The World's Work,* September 1922, p. 547.

8. *School and Society,* vol. XVIII, no. 460 (October 20, 1923), p. 464.

9. Quoted in "Yale's Movie Version of American History," *Literary Digest,* vol. LXXII, no. 9 (March 4, 1922), p. 43.

10. Arthur Edwin Krows, "Motion Pictures—Not for Theatres," *Educational Screen,* vol. XXI, no. 3 (March 1942), p. 106.

11. Arthur Edwin Krows, "Motion Pictures—Not for Theatres," *Educational Screen,* vol. XXI, no. 4 (April 1942), p. 138.

12. Laura Kay Palmer, *Osgood and Anthony Perkins* (Jefferson, N.C.: McFarland, 1991).

13. Quotes are taken from the original publicity brochure on the Chronicles of America, in the Margaret Herrick Library of the Academy of Motion Picture Arts and Sciences.

14. Arthur Edwin Krows, "Motion Pictures—Not for Theatres," *Educational Screen,* vol. XXI, no. 4 (April 1942), p. 139.

15. Ibid.

SEVEN

The 1930s and 1940s

The introduction of the sound motion picture dominated both the theatrical and the non-theatrical film fields in the 1930s, and the course of the history of the latter was largely influenced by the pioneer in the introduction of sound to film, the Western Electric Company. The company had acquired the necessary components for the "talkies" to enhance its Bell Telephone system, but Western Electric was not unaware of the potential of sound films and experimented with both sound-on-film and sound-on-disc motion pictures in the 1920s. Although sound-on-film was ultimately adopted by the film industry, the first commercially successful "talkie" was the 1927 Al Jolson vehicle *The Jazz Singer*, utilizing sound-on-disc provided by Western Electric.

To market its non–telephone-related products, in 1927 Western Electric created a new company, Electrical Research Products, Inc. (ERPI), which licensed the use of sound equipment and also provided acoustical engineering advice to those in the industry. In March 1929, ERPI founded a non-theatrical division to promote the use of sound in religious, educational, and other non-commercial film projects. The following year, the ERPI staff led by Frederick L. Devereux and Dr. V. C. Arnspiger began production on a series of 35mm sound-on-film shorts dealing with athletics, social sciences and vocational guidance. Unfortunately few if any schools were equipped with 35mm sound-on-film projection equipment; and until 1934, when 16mm sound-on-film projectors were introduced, ERPI took a step back and began production of films utilizing sound-on-disc.

In part because of the lack of sound projection equipment at non-theatrical locations, ERPI decided to provide its own, offering "road show licenses" and providing portable equipment and projectionists to sponsors and producers of non-theatrical releases. The first four independent road show distributors/exhibitors were licensed in 1932, with the first licensee being William "Bill" McCallum, who was to join ERPI in 1937. As Robert Finehout noted, these ERPI licensees "went from Main Street to main stem with their projectors, loudspeakers, screens and cans of film. They set up shop in auditoriums, grange halls, dealer showrooms, factories, even out-of-doors where farmers and townspeople gathered to see 'talking pictures.' For many it was their first talkie."[1]

By 1934, the ERPI licensees were able to offer either 35mm or 16mm sound-on-film presentations. The audiences for many ERPI presentations in the 1930s were substantial: 17,500 people in Raleigh, North Carolina, viewed the Ford Motor Company's *These Thirty Years*; films celebrating A&P's birthday in Madison Square Garden attracted an audience of 20,000; 4,200 people, more than half the population of Orangeburg, South Carolina, witnessed a B.F. Goodrich program; and 13,000 at Philadelphia's Convention Hall watched the Ford Motor Company's *Rhapsody in Steel*. The H.J. Heinz Company, Brown and Williamson Tobacco Corporation, the National Association of Manufacturers, Weyerhauser, the Institute of Life Insurance, American Iron & Steel, and the Metropolitan Life Insurance Company were just a few of ERPI's clients, with Metropolitan's film campaign for health education presented by ERPI garnering a total audience of more than fifteen million.

Frank Arlinghaus, who was then sales manager of ERPI's Distribution Division, recalled, "Auditorium type showings were really big time, with the Distribution Division not only providing equipment but uniformed (yes, uniformed) operators and 'local advertising, publicity and merchandising tie-ups.' At these shows each person who attended was asked to fill in and sign a card. 'One of our clients says his best prospect list is still the signed tickets turned in at last year's consumer shows,' the brochure exclaimed."[2]

In 1935, the first ten ERPI licensees gathered in New York, and after rejecting the name of "Community Talking Picture Service," decided to adopt the trade name "Modern Talking Picture Service." A tombstone trademark and the slogan "any place, any time" were also adopted. A year later, Arlinghaus was named ERPI's first distribution manager, and the company began the theatrical release of some of its films.

ERPI might have continued as a household name almost to the present had it not been for the 1937 decision of the Federal Communications Commission to require that Western Electric's parent company AT&T

divest itself of a number of its non–telephone-related companies. As a result of that decision, a number of new concerns were created. Western Electric's industrial film production became Audio Productions; the educational films division was renamed Encyclopaedia Britannica Films; sound equipment for theatres was now manufactured by Altec-Lansing, "The Voice of the Theater"; and continuous music in the home, office, and supermarket was provided by Muzak.

Frank Arlinghaus was able to arrange that employees of the distribution department take over ERPI, with his becoming its first president and the company renamed Modern Talking Picture Service. Now with thirty-five licensees, Modern continued providing projection equipment, but it was obvious that more and more locations were acquiring their own 16mm projectors. In February 1937, Modern offered its first 16mm release, available for booking at self-equipped 16mm locations, the American Iron & Steel Institute's *Steel—A Symphony on Industry*. In 1942, with twenty-eight titles in its library, Modern decided to change the thrust of its operation and become a distributor of educational, industrial, and sponsored films. As part of the war effort, in 1943 Modern became principal distributor of industrial incentive films for the army's Industrial Service Division.

Opening branch offices throughout the United States, Modern Talking Picture Service dominated the sponsored-film distribution field in the 1940s. It embraced early television as a potential market for sponsored films, particularly as few entertainment features were available to the new medium. Carl Lenz, who became Modern's president with the death of Frank Arlinghaus in 1964, explained, "Stations were faced with a serious programming problem: lack of product. Also, original live production was difficult, what with the limitations of equipment, talent, and know-how. Sponsored films were available in comparative abundance and, of course, they were free. The rush was on and soon distributors were gearing up to satisfy the voracious appetites of television programmers."[3]

The 1969 acquisition of Modern Talking Picture Service by the Cincinnati-based KDI Corporation had little initial impact on the company. In 1978, it formed a subsidiary, ModernCinema 35, to distribute short subjects to theatres, making available efforts by young filmmakers funded by the National Endowment for the Arts to a wider audience. That same year, Radio City Music Hall presented twenty-three consecutive weeks of short films from Modern Talking Picture Service. Unlike many of its contemporaries from what might be called "the golden age" of the non-theatrical film, Modern was able to survive by embracing video distribution. Throughout its seven decades of existence, it has shown a remarkable ability to change in step with changes in the industry.[4]

The 1937 FCC decision that gave birth to the Modern Talking Picture Service also created a giant in the educational film production and distribution field, Encyclopaedia Britannica Films, Inc. Three years earlier, the reference work *The Encyclopaedia Britannica* (which was first published in 1771) had become affiliated with the University of Chicago, through the financial generosity of William B. Benton (1900–1973).

William Benton was a multimillionaire philanthropist, who founded the advertising agency of Benton & Bowles and was a Connecticut senator from 1949 to 1953. Following the decision that AT&T must dispose of ERPI Classroom Films, Inc., Benton drew up a recommendation for the Rockefeller Foundation to acquire the company through a $4 million deal and convert it to a non-profit venture. The proposal was rejected.

In 1943, again through Benton's efforts, the University of Chicago acquired total control of the Encyclopaedia company from its previous owner, Sears, Roebuck and Company. Appointed board chairman of Encyclopaedia Britannica, Benton once more turned his interest toward ERPI Classroom Films, Inc., which Western Electric was still trying to dispose of. Benton was able to negotiate a deal with Western Electric's financial vice president Kennedy Stevenson whereby Encyclopaedia Britannica would acquire ERPI for $1 million, payable over a ten-year period; in November 1943, ERPI had a new owner.

In a prepared statement, Benton commented,

> When Sears, Roebuck and Company made the gift of Encyclopaedia Britannica, Inc., the university welcomed it not only because of the worldwide importance of the Encyclopaedia Britannica itself, but also because the Britannica organization offered facilities for extending the university's educational ventures in other fields. The purchase of ERPI Films is a natural and logical phase of this extension of Britannica as an educational organization allied to the university. . . .
>
> Association of the university with ERPI may result not only in expansion of production of films for classroom use, but also in expansion in other types of educational films used outside the classroom. The university's relationship to the enterprise will be confined to making its educational knowledge and staff available to the ERPI organization.[5]

E. E. Schumaker continued as president and chief executive officer of the renamed ERPI Classroom Films, Inc., and Benton was appointed chairman of the board of Encyclopaedia Britannica Films, a position he held after the company was renamed Encyclopaedia Educational Corporation in 1966 and until his death. Early in 1944, the Eastman Kodak Company turned over 250 silent films from the Eastman Teaching Films collection, a gift that further enhanced the prominence of the new company in the educational film field. The company even embarked on a project to provide specially edited versions of some of its titles, in 8mm and 16mm, for the home movie market in 1948. Utilizing studio facilities in the Chicago suburb of Wilmette, Encyclopaedia Britannica Films produced an astonishing number of titles: 373 in the 1940s, 475 in the 1950s, and 433 in the 1960s.

Herman Kogan explained the production process: "Each film is designed for use in teaching and is so made that students can learn faster and better with it than without it. Consequently, great care in production and preparation is taken. Before a film is begun, researchers go over the full field of texts and courses on the specified subject. Curriculum specialists are consulted for advice, and every movie is made under the supervision of an associate in research and production and with the guidance of an expert or a scholar."[6]

Profits from the sale of the films were apparently negligible with "no significant returns and no dividends on the several millions of dollars invested,"[7] but there were ancillary uses for the films, including the use of stills therefrom as illustrations for books published by Encyclopaedia Britannica Press.

The University of Chicago took the making of Encyclopaedia Britannica films very seriously. Stephen M. Carey, an advisor to the organization and professor of educational psychology at the university, explained to the industry trade paper *Boxoffice* (August 5, 1944) that "Encyclopaedia Britannica Films will not release any pictures to schools that distort incidents or characters for the sake of entertainment. . . . Most of the Disney cartoons intended for the educational field are not acceptable to Encyclopaedia Britannica Films because they place entertainment above authenticity." Referring to a U.S. government–sponsored film produced by Disney for South American audiences to warn of the danger of malarial infection from mosquitoes, Carey said, "Teachers cannot accept the film for schools because it employs distortions in aiming at the concluding point. A mosquito must be presented as an authentic mosquito, even though Disney's form of a mosquito may be the more entertaining one. We cannot afford to show before children anything but a true picture of the mosquitoes. The mosquito can be enlarged for the purpose of clarification, but none of its members nor its shape can be distorted."

Nor was Encyclopaedia Britannica Films the first direct involvement in non-theatrical film production by the University of Chicago. In 1935 the university's Oriental Institute produced *The Human Adventure*, under the supervision of Dr. James Henry Breasted. First seen at New York's Carnegie Hall on October 29, 1935, the film was a record of the Oriental Institute's fourteen archaeological expeditions to Persia, Palestine, Syria, Anatolia, Egypt, and Iraq.

The *New York Times* (October 30, 1935) reviewed the feature-length production and coincidentally presented a prevalent and recurring crit-

icism of educational films: "Although the picture falls within the un-
happy category known as 'educational films,' it is nevertheless entertaining in a full sense: a pictorial counterpart to the early chapters of an
Outline of History and a skillfully edited and well-told story of some
ancient adventures that are just coming to life today."

As enthusiastic as Benton about the value of educational films was
David A. Smart (1892–1952). Described by one of his friends and colleagues as "a born salesman, an idea man and an entrepreneur,"[8] Smart
formed his own company, the David A. Smart Publishing Company, in
1921; in January 1934 he began publication of his best-known magazine,
Esquire, followed on November 23, 1936, by *Coronet*. One of Smart's
hobbies was amateur movie-making with which he was so besotted that
he even built his own studio on the grounds of his estate in the Chicago
suburb of Glenview. (The size of the studio complex is evidenced by its
being taken over during the war for making training films for the U.S.
Navy.) Among Smart's amateur efforts was a film presenting the beauty
of the children's photographs of Nell Dorr, which had often graced the
pages of *Coronet*.

Smart early recognized the value of film as an informational medium,
pointing out that in 1933 in Germany some 16,000 16mm projectors were
in use. In 1940, he established Coronet Productions to service the needs
of the educational and informational film market, with one of its first
releases being *Aptitudes and Occupations* (1941). The company was renamed Coronet Instructional Film Division of Esquire, Inc., in 1944. In
1949, Coronet acquired a 62 percent controlling interest (the percentage
owned by chairman of the board Marion Harvey and vice president S. J.
Sperberg) in Ideal Pictures Corporation for a reported $50,000.

Like Encyclopaedia Britannica Films, Coronet was careful always to
use experts in the field as advisors and consultants on each of its productions, always crediting them as such in the credits of the films.
According to John Mercer, Coronet sent "staff members to national and
regional meetings of educators and other professionals as a way of keep-
ing abreast of developments in education. The company also has staff
members who examine new textbooks and the curriculum guides of
cities and states."[9] Despite the lack of a constant demand for color motion
pictures on educational subjects, Coronet shot every one of its films in
color but through 1975 released them in both color and black-and-white
versions. By that time the demand was exclusively for color, against
which the cost of black-and-white was beginning to be equal.

The 1970s was a decade of continued expansion for Coronet, long
recognized as "one of the nation's leading producers of 16mm educational motion pictures."[10] In 1973, the company sold its one millionth
print and organized a new subsidiary, Perspective Films, whose first
releases dealt with the art of the motion picture.

There were, of course, other educational film libraries in competition with Encyclopaedia Britannica and Coronet. In the spring of 1934, the Harvard Film Service was established, taking over the activities of the University Film Foundation, created in 1928 to produce, rent, and sell educational films. These productions from Harvard were made in co-operation with Pathé, and released through the Educational Department of the Pathé Exchange, Inc. One of the first titles was *Houses of the Arctic and the Tropics* in the Pathé-Harvard Human Geography series. All the films were available for rental, and they could also be purchased by schools for $35 per 400 ft. (ten-minute) reel.

The Motion Picture Producers and Distributors of America was founded in 1922 as a liaison organization between the film industry and the public and was originally headed by Will H. Hays. (In 1945, the name was changed to the current one, Motion Picture Association of America.) As early as 1922, the group financed the work of a special committee, created in association with the National Education Association, to survey theatrical films that might be suitable for adaptation to school use. In 1929, the Motion Picture Producers and Distributors of America compiled a survey on the potential use of sound films in education and hosted a conference of several hundred college presidents and educators. As an outgrowth of that conference the Committee on Social Values in Motion Pictures was created. It reviewed various feature films and received permission to extract clips from eight, which were edited together in 1933 as an educational subject titled *Secrets of Success*.

In the spring of 1937 the Motion Picture Producers and Distributors of America invited a group of educators to form an Advisory Committee on the Use of Motion Pictures in Education. The committee recommended making significant theatrical features available at nominal cost to educational institutions and without financial return to the cooperating producers. As a result of these recommendations, Teaching Film Custodians was incorporated in 1938 in New York as a non-profit educational service organization. Its founding board was James Rowland Angell (president of Yale University), Frederick H. Blair (Department of Education, State of New York), Isaiah Bowman (president of Johns Hopkins University), Karl T. Compton (president of the Massachusetts Institute of Technology), Edmund E. Day (president of Cornell University), Royal B. Farnum (executive vice president of the Rhode Island School of Design), Willard E. Givens (executive secretary of the National Education Association), Jay F. Nash (executive secretary of the New York State Association for Health, Physical Education and Recreation), A. L. Thelkeld (Superintendent of Schools, Denver, Colorado, and Montclair, New Jersey), and Mark A. May (director of the Institute of Human Relations at Yale University), who served as the new organization's president from 1938–1968.

Rather than release entire features from participating companies, including RKO, M-G-M, Warner Bros., and 20th Century-Fox, Teaching Film Custodians produced condensations that often emphasized a certain portion of the storyline and substantially changed the plot. For example, the twenty-four minute Teaching Film Custodians release from 1953, *First Seize His Books*, is a condensation of the 1940 M-G-M feature *The Mortal Storm*. The original production was anti-Nazi, but the condensation produced at the height of the Cold War is able to make communism the enemy.

The first catalog from Teaching Film Custodians was issued on July 1, 1939. Following a three-year trial period, agreements between the Motion Picture Producers and Distributors of America and Teaching Film Custodians were renewed in 1943. The renewal was no surprise in that the film industry was well aware of the valuable public relations exercise in which it was involved. On April 17, 1942, the Motion Picture Producers and Distributors of America released a press release, through Associated Press, stating:

> Today's youngsters are learning their school lessons from teachers Gable and Garson.
>
> Clark and Greer—and hundreds of other top Hollywood stars—have been teaching school for four years now. Their classroom roles may be as important as any they've ever played.
>
> For youngsters in up-to-date English classes, Professor Gable acts out *Mutiny on the Bounty*. Miss Garson renders *Pride and Prejudice*. Mickey Rooney interprets Mark Twain's *Huckleberry Finn*. Norma Shearer shows what Shakespeare had in mind with *Romeo and Juliet*.

Further emphasizing its concern for education, the Motion Picture Association of America, as the organization had become by that time, established an Educational Services Department at its Washington, D.C., headquarters in 1946, with Roger Albright as its director. The department merged with Teaching Film Custodians in 1958.

In the 1950s, Teaching Film Custodians began releasing television productions for school use, and in 1952 it sponsored a self-promotion documentary, *The TFC Story*. A few years later, E.I. DuPont de Nemours Company donated the educational rights to seventy television films in the "Cavalcade of America" series (seen first on NBC and later ABC from 1952 to 1957) to Teaching Film Custodians. In 1960, Teaching Film Custodians began production of filmstrips for classroom and community group use, beginning with a fifty-frame color filmstrip, with script based on the 1959 M-G-M production of *Ben-Hur*. Teaching Film Custodians was merged with the Audio Visual Center at Indiana University in May 1973.

Aside from its work with Teaching Film Custodians, the Motion Picture Producers and Distributors of America was involved in one other major non-theatrical activity, which was the sponsorship of the feature-length *Land of Liberty* for the 1939 New York World's Fair. Supervised by Cecil B. DeMille, the film told the history of America by utilizing clips from extant Hollywood productions, as "old" as James Cruze's *The Covered Wagon* (1923) and as recent as *The Plainsman* (1936). The film was screened at no charge for visitors to the fair, and a revised and shortened version that included clips from *Abe Lincoln in Illinois* (1939) and *Northwest Passage* (1940) was presented at the reopened 1940 fair. In April 1940, the Motion Picture Producers and Distributors of America unanimously agreed to make the film available, on a non-theatrical basis, to schools, civic groups, and other non-profit organizations. A 16mm version was also prepared for classroom use.

Land of Liberty is not the only record of Cecil B. DeMille's interest in non-theatrical filmmaking. Early in 1946, he announced the formation of the Cecil B. DeMille Pictures Corporation, which was to make 16mm educational, religious, and industrial films, but nothing appears to have come of the proposal.

Aside from Teaching Film Custodians, other companies were involved in similar activities. In 1941, Nu-Art Films, Inc., released in 16mm four versions of D.W. Griffith's 1930 feature *Abraham Lincoln: The Entire Life and Career of Abraham Lincoln* (ninety minutes), *The Private and Public Life of Abraham Lincoln* (sixty minutes), *The Public Life of Abraham Lincoln* (thirty minutes), and *Highlights of Lincoln's Career* (eleven minutes).

Early in 1937, for classroom use only, Paramount produced a series of one-reel condensations of its features, which were released for sale or rental by Bell & Howell and for rental only by Films Inc. The 1937 Claudette Colbert feature, *Maid of Salem*, became *Seeing Salem*, an educational view of life in an eighteenth-century New England town. From the same year, the musical *High, Wide and Handsome* provided a study of the pioneer oil-drilling industry in Pennsylvania as *Men and Oil*, while *Wells Fargo* provided students with a view of the westward expansion of the United States in *Wheels of Empire*.

In 1975, Learning Corporation of America, the 16mm educational division of Screen Gems, Inc., which was, in turn, the television division of Columbia Pictures, released a series of thirty-minute condensations of Columbia features available for both rental and sale. Each film included a commentary by Orson Welles, and the series was accompanied by a 110-page teachers manual. Each feature was retitled for the 16mm truncated release. *The Caine Mutiny* (1954) was issued as *Authority and Rebellion; Lord Jim* (1965) as *Heroes and Cowards; A Man for All Seasons* (1966) as *Conscience in Conflict; The Taming of the Shrew* (1967) as *Man and Woman; In Cold Blood* (1967) as *Crime and the Criminal;* and *Macbeth* (1971) as *Power and Corruption.*

The Hollywood film industry first recognized 16mm as an alternate distribution method in the summer of 1929, when Universal established a non-theatrical department in New York. It would handle not only Universal's features and short subjects but also its newsreel production. Early in 1931, Columbia opened a non-theatrical division headed by S.S. Liggett. Neither department appears to have had much impact, and their activities were gradually phased out by the studios. The value of the 16mm market received new acknowledgment in the summer of 1945, when M-G-M appointed Orton Hicks to head a 16mm department. The studio released its features and short subjects in 16mm throughout the world, with the exception of the United States, and it was not until 1956 that a limited selection of M-G-M films became available in 16mm to American schools. At the beginning of 1946, RKO became the second studio to distribute its films worldwide in 16mm, but again the arrangement ignored the American market.

The non-theatrical film industry did provide gainful employment for many whose careers had begun with its more senior commercial brother. After her Hollywood career petered out in the mid-1930s, former silent star Virginia Brown Faire recalled moving to Chicago to work in both radio and non-theatrical films; other actors from the silent era whom she encountered included Cullen Landis, Allan Forrest, and Jason Robards.[11] Typical of the films attracting former Hollywood actors is *Meet the Watkins Family*, produced in 1940 by Roland Reed for the National Carbon Company and starring Ralph Morgan, Andy Clyde, and Raymond Hatton.

Edwin Carewe had been a prominent director of silent films, including *Resurrection* (1927), *Ramona* (1928), and *Evangeline* (1929). With his theatrical career over, in 1934 the director formed Edwin Carewe Pictures Corporation, "for the purpose of producing, distributing and exhibiting clean, worthwhile entertainment and educational pictures to schools, colleges, women's federations, churches and fraternal organizations."[12] His first production was *Are We Civilized?*, described by Variety (June 19, 1934) as "a morally high preachment for world peace that loses its point through having selected the wrong medium of expression. As a picture the commendable argument will hardly convince more than a few, because it's not likely that more than a few will see it." The film featured former silent star William Farnum and Anita Louise and received its Hollywood premiere at the Beverly Christian Church on November 17, 1935.

At least two Hollywood actors became involved in non-theatrical production. In December 1945, *Film News* reported that Richard Dix (who had been nominated for an Academy Award for his 1931 performance in *Cimarron*) had purchased a site on the Sunset Strip on which he planned to erect a small studio for non-theatrical production.[13] In 1946,

Eddie Albert formed Albert Films, in association with John Fletcher, for the production of educational and industrial subjects.

Among the Hollywood actors to be seen in non-theatrical productions were Ralph Bellamy in *It's All Yours* (1946), produced by Willard Pictures for Pocket Books; Lyle Talbot, in *The House That Faith Built* (1950), produced by Wilding Picture Productions for Anheuser-Busch; Thomas Mitchell in *Dear Mr. Editor* (1953), produced by Galbreath Picture Productions for National Homes; Tony Randall in *You Are There, Too* (1954), produced by Owen Murphy Productions for the Prudential Insurance Company; and Ronald Reagan in *Hands We Trust* (1959), produced by Fred A. Niles Productions for the National College of Surgeons. In 1957, Nils Asther ended his career as an actor by becoming special representative for the non-theatrical concern of Louis W. Kellman Productions. And in November 1949, *Business Screen* ran an advertisement for narrators available to non-theatrical producers; among the half-dozen featured speakers was Myron L. Wallace, better known to viewers of *60 Minutes* for the past twenty or so years as Mike Wallace.

Nor was involvement in non-theatrical films limited to personalities from the world of Hollywood movie-making. As early as 1939, two major literary figures of the day, Marc Connelly and Franklin P. Adams, visited the Astoria Studios in New York to appear in a film concerning the advertising salesman and the space buyer, sponsored by *The New Yorker*.

One company that enjoyed phenomenal growth in the 1930s was Castle Films. Founded in 1924 by Eugene W. Castle (1897–1960), with an investment of $10,000, the company grew to be one of the largest suppliers of 8mm and 16mm short subjects and feature condensations to the home market. Eugene Castle entered the film industry before 1920 as a newsreel cameraman and later began producing industrial shorts for the United Fruit Company and California Fruit Growers Exchange. According to Arthur Edwin Krows, Castle began his business by distributing educational and industrial films free to schools, with the sponsors picking up the cost. He guaranteed such sponsors an eventual audience of two million for their films. "When the given film has reached the two million mark," wrote Krows, "Castle destroys the subject, including all prints. Consequently, no subject in his list is more than three years of age, clients are disposed to make new subjects, and school teachers, thus unusually assured of comparative freshness of information, are stimulated to ask for his reels while they are available."[14]

While other companies saw the non-theatrical market as concerned primarily with rental, Castle had the foresight in 1936 to realize that the more projectors sold, the greater would be the need by users for at least a limited number of films that would remain their property. His first release, in 16mm only, was of the coronation of King George VI. It was followed by 16mm and 8mm versions of the Hindenburg disaster, and it was claimed that an astonishing 120,000 copies of this film were sold as novelty items in drug stores, department stores and toy shops.

Many of Castle's choices for release were obvious. For $3.00 (16mm) and $1.00 (8mm), it was possible to purchase "The Star Spangled Banner," "recorded on film, and heard in conjunction with a stirring, movie presentation of patriotism."[15] As with many of Castle's releases, the company's publicity urged, "Cut this footage into films you already own." Another popular release was the annual *News Parade*, a ten-minute compilation of newsreel clips documenting world news from 1937 onward. A complementary series was *Football Thrills*, with brief scenes from college football games.

Scenics, actuality shorts, and Terrytoon cartoons comprised the bulk of Castle's offerings, with prices in the early 1940s varying according to length. A full ten-minute reel in 16mm was $17.50, compared to $5.50 in 8mm. But many of the Castle releases ran only three minutes, priced at $2.75 in 16mm and $1.75 in 8mm. The Second World War provided a bonanza for Castle Films, which was able to offer innumerable short subjects that not only enabled its customers to "keep your records of the wars complete" but also provided footage of battles fought by friends and loved ones: *Bombs over Europe, British-Greek Victories, Britain's Commandos in Action, America's Call to Arms, Japs Bomb U.S.A.!, Bombing of Pearl Harbor!/Burning of "S.S. Normandie"!, Russia Stops Hitler, Fight for Rome!/Russia's Mighty Offensive!, Yanks Smash Truk!,* and *Italy Surrenders.* The exclamation mark was the most important and ongoing aspect of the Castle titles!

In 1946, Universal Pictures acquired the Filmosound Library and used it as the basis for United World, Inc., which was to be the studio's new 16mm distribution outlet. A year later, Universal purchased Castle Films, which was boasting a total gross income to date of $130 million. Universal continued to operate Castle Films well into the 1970s, keeping to Eugene Castle's original policy of selling interest and news shorts but also adding ten-minute compilations of some of the studio's feature films starring W.C. Fields, Abbott and Costello, Lon Chaney, Jr., and others.

In 1946, Castle Films began marketing "Castle Music Albums," which were nothing more than three different examples of Soundies combined in a nine-minute reel. Soundies were short, three-minute musical numbers produced in the early 1940s for presentation on film jukeboxes called Panorams. In that they were presented for profit, with the listener/viewer paying for the privilege, Soundies were not non-theatrical films. The Castle release of them was non-theatrical, as was an earlier offering of the films for rental and/or sale by Walter O. Gutlohn, Inc., in 1942. Two years after the first of the Castle Films release of the Soundies, the company's major competitor, Official Films, Inc., began releasing Soundies in groups of three titled "Musical Film Revues." (During the next decade, Blackhawk Films was to sell literally hundreds of thousands of Soundies not in newly manufactured prints as did Castle and Official but in the form of the original prints used in the Panoram machines.)[16]

Like Castle Films, Official Films, Inc., discovered the home non-theatrical market in the 1930s. Initially organized in 1939 to produce instructional, sponsored, and entertainment shorts for outright sale in 16mm, Official Films quickly discovered a more lucrative market in 16mm and 8mm prints of early public-domain Charlie Chaplin shorts, to which the company added music and sound effects. The company's founder, Leslie Winik, entered independent production in 1945 and sold Official Films to a syndicate headed by George A. Hirliman, Harry J. Rothman, and Aaron Katz. The trio expanded the company's business, listing some three hundred titles for sale by 1948 and publishing a booklet on "The Film Rental Library," which explained to print purchasers how they might use such films as the basis for a local rental library.

In 1922, *The Educational Screen* observed that "When an American school child watches a screen, 99 times out of 100, it is a theatrical screen."[17] The numbers might not have changed drastically in the next twenty years, but change they most certainly did. A survey in May 1940 by the Motion Picture Division, Bureau of Foreign and Domestic Commerce, Department of Commerce, showed that 6,059 silent 16mm projectors and 6,384 sound 16mm projectors were in use in American colleges and high schools. Providing films for those projectors were an estimated 350 producers of educational, documentary, industrial, and religious films in the United States alone, as well as many foreign production houses with American offices, notably the aggressive and well-organized British Ministry of Information.

In an effort to organize the non-theatrical film industry and provide it with a single voice, in 1939 William K. Hedwig, president of Nu-Art Films, Inc., organized the Allied Non-Theatrical Film Association. The association's first president was Bertram Willoughby of Ideal Pictures Corporation.

America's entry into the Second World War provided a major boost for non-theatrical film production and underlined the prominence that the U.S. government could command in the field through its various film production activities.

The work of the Department of Agriculture is discussed in chapter 4. Next in pioneering importance was the Department of Interior's Bureau of Mines, established by an act of Congress on February 25, 1913. The act read in part that one of the Bureau's duties was to "disseminate information covering these subjects in such manner as will best carry out the purpose of the act." Far-sighted government bureaucrats determined that the wording meant that the bureau might become involved in the production of educational and informational films, and, under the guidance of Morton F. Leopold, the agency made its first film in 1916. In the 1920s, it established a major educational film program, relying for funding not on Congressional appropriations but on private industry, which was anxious to promote its activities in the field. In 1940, it was reported that the mineral and allied industries had provided more than $1 million to the bureau for the production and distribution of films, none of which directly advertised or promoted a product or company. By 1945, some eight million people had viewed the films of the U.S. Bureau of Mines. Its most popular title, *First Steps in First Aid* (1943), was distributed 2,989 times and seen by 332,000 people.

Rather than slowing down non-theatrical growth, the Second World War encouraged economic expansion, as more and more producers became involved in war-oriented government production. Beginning in November 1941, Castle Films, Inc. began releasing Office of Education training films produced by its Division of Visual Aids. The physical production of such films was handled by eight major non-theatrical producers: Audio Productions, Inc., Bray Studios, Inc., Jamieson Film Company, the Jam Handy Organization, Herbert Keskow, Ted Nemeth, Pathescope Company of America, Inc., and Tradefilms, Inc. Burton Holmes Films, Inc., was not among the group because it was far too busy between 1942 and 1945 producing forty-seven films for the Navy Training Film Branch, and the company's laboratory was able to boast that by May 1945 it had processed more than twenty-eight million feet of release prints for the army and navy.

By 1943, both the army and the navy were using more 16mm film in the production of training films than the entire Hollywood film industry. That same year, the Bureau of Motion Pictures of the Office of War Information decided to create a National 16mm Motion Picture Advisory and Policy Committee, to determine "the most effective production and utilization of 16mm films in disseminating war information."[18] The action might seem somewhat unnecessary in view of the Bureau's already having captured an audience of fifty million for its 16mm releases between June 1942 and June 1943. However, a committee was formed, with representatives from the Educational Film Library Association, the Audio Visual Aid Committee of the American Library Association, the National University Extension Association, Departments of Visual Instruction of the National Education Association, the Allied Non-Theatrical Film Association, the National Association of Visual Education Dealers, the National War Committee for the Visual Education Industry, and the Visual Equipment Manufacturers Association.

There was something of a change in non-theatrical production in the 1940s, as some sponsors tried to get away from the look of an industrial film toward a more lyrical documentary approach. The most obvious example is the Standard Oil Company of New Jersey's sponsorship of veteran documentary filmmaker Robert Flaherty's production of *Louisiana Story*. The only screen credit to either Standard Oil or Esso is a brief acknowledgment in the titles to the "Humble Oil Derrick Crew," Humble Oil being an Esso subsidiary.

Filmed between 1946 and 1948, *Louisiana Story* uses a minimal amount of dialogue and a surfeit of music by Virgil Thomson to study the swamps and bayous of Louisiana through the eyes of a young Cajun boy. It is perhaps most remarkable for its refusal to endorse the sponsor's oil drilling in the swamps. The drilling is seen to bring security and moderate prosperity to the boy's family, but it has changed the way of life there forever, to which the boy responds by spitting in the water.

The point was perhaps lost on both the sponsor and the audience. *Variety* (September 22, 1948) commented, "Besides being excellent entertainment, *Louisiana Story* should be invaluable public relations material for Standard Oil of N.J., which contributed the necessary $200,000 production coin to Flaherty. The firm has no rights and no identification in the film, but stands to get across the idea that oil companies are beneficently public-spirited, their employees honest, industrious and amiable, and their operations productive and innocuous."

In 1945, the non-profit International Film Foundation was created in New York, with an initial two-year grant of $300,000 from Darvella Mills Foundation of Montclair, New Jersey, and with another veteran documentary filmmaker Julien Bryan (1899–1974) as its head. "Dedicated to the building of world understanding through the production and distribution of documentary films,"[19] the foundation's first productions dealt with Russia and Poland.

A change in outlook for non-theatrical production was urged by distinguished Scottish filmmaker John Grierson, who had founded the National Film Board of Canada, that country's leading theatrical and non-theatrical filmmaker, in 1939. Arguing that the cost of 16mm projectors would go down from a current 1944 price of $350 to $150, Grierson pointed out that they could become available to any group, which would lead to "more seating capacity outside of the theatres than there is inside of them." He continued:

"This non-theatrical audience is today being organized on a vast scale in all progressive countries. It represents a revolution in both the film industry and in education. It demands films concerned with education of every kind, professional and civic. It needs films concerned with the real interests of people and the provisions of materials which make for a creative citizenship. Its potential development is enormous."[20]

The increased availability of 16mm projection equipment coupled with the realization that non-theatrical films could be accepted both on aesthetic and artistic levels helped expand the film society movement in the United States. Film societies had been an accepted area of film appre-

ciation in Europe since the 1920s. One of the first prominent American
film societies was Cinema 16, founded in New York in 1947 by Amos
Vogel, who was later to become a leader in the independent film movement. In an article in *Film News*, Vogel explained:

"Cinema 16 was created by a small group of individuals interested in
the advancement of the motion picture, who felt they had waited long
enough for others to do what was clearly imperative: to create a showcase
for outstanding documentary and fact films, to bridge the gap between
such film production and its vast potential audience.

"Cinema 16's purpose is two-fold. It will not only present artistically
satisfying films to the public but will awaken people to a greater understanding of their world by presentation of socially purposeful documentary films."[21]

Cinema 16 presented its first program to an audience of 200 at the
Provincetown Playhouse in October 1947. It ceased operations in 1963.

It was not the first American film society. Writing in the *New York
Times* (September 18, 1949), Thomas Pryor reported that "Since the war,
somewhere in the neighbourhood of 200 film societies have been organized by persons whose interest in the film medium goes beyond the
purely entertainment functions of the commercial theatre." In April 1954,
a Film Society Caucus was formed at the American Film Assembly, and
the following year the American Federation of Film Societies was established. For the next two decades the federation tried to coordinate the
interests of American film societies, whose number had grown to 4,000
by 1965, but it became more and more political in later years, as its
executive director William A. Starr continued a critical campaign, which
was far from unjustified, against the American Film Institute; the federation disappeared from the scene in the 1970s.

In March 1941, 16mm cinematographers organized as the Society of
16mm Cinematographers, headquartered in and with virtually all of its
members active in the Los Angeles area. A new trade paper for the
16mm industry, *Film World*, began publication in 1945; and in 1948 it
launched the annual *Film World 16mm Film and Industry Directory*, the
first and only major 16mm trade annual modeled after the 35mm theatrical film industry's *International Motion Picture Almanac*. A further boost
came in December 1946 when the National Board of Review of Motion
Pictures announced that regularly it would review non-theatrical films.

Also in 1946, the Industrial Audio-Visual Association was founded
"To study all means of audio-visual communications including creation,
production, appreciation, use and distribution; to promote better standards and equipment and to establish a high concept of ethics in the
relations of members with associated interests."

The most prominent organization formed in the 1940s and the one
that continues to dominate the non-theatrical film scene was the Edu-

cational Film Library Association (EFLA). EFLA has its origins in the Educational Film Lending Library Council, formed at a meeting on March 27, 1942, by representatives from eleven institutions with educational film libraries located in Chicago. According to L. C. Larson, chairman of the committee, "a number of county and city school systems and public libraries and museums asked it to extend the scope of its representation to include all educational film libraries."[22] A meeting was held in Washington, D.C., in October 1942, and a month later a proposed plan for an Educational Film Library Association was sent to the directors of approximately 150 film libraries. Correspondence continued, and on March 17–18, 1943, the first meeting of an elected board of directors was held in Chicago, at which time it was agreed that the American Film Center would serve as the administrative office of the association and that the American Film Center's director, Donald Slesinger, would become the association's acting administrative director. The Educational Film Library Association was formally incorporated on April 13, 1943.

L. C. Larson, who was instrumental in the creation of EFLA, took a leave of absence from Indiana University to become its first full-time administrative director, and Elizabeth Harding was named executive secretary. She was succeeded in April 1946 by Emily S. Jones, who remained with EFLA until her retirement as administrative director in 1969. Almost concurrently with Jones' appointment, the Rockefeller Foundation, which had provided a grant for EFLA's foundation, withdrew its financial support; and the organization survived only thanks to help from Julien Bryan and the International Film Foundation, with whom EFLA shared accommodation.

Emily S. Jones recalled, "Those early post-war years were arduous but exciting. It was always a cliff-hanging possibility that EFLA would not survive, but somehow we always managed. The whole AV [audiovisual] field was starting up fresh; the people who had founded it in the Thirties were now the old-timers, and new people were appearing, many of them out of service in the armed forces."[23]

NOTES

1. Robert Finehout, "Sponsored Film: Talking Pictures to Satellite Transmission," *Business & Home TV Screen*, November 1978, p. 18.

2. Ibid.

3. Ibid., p. 19.

4. Modern Talking Picture Service, Inc., is currently located at 5000 Park Street North, St. Petersburg, FL 33709.

5. Quoted in *School and Society*, vol. LVIII, no. 1512 (December 18, 1947), p. 469.

6. Herman Kogan, *The Great EB: The Story of the Encyclopaedia Britannica* (Chicago: University of Chicago Press, 1958), p. 262.

7. Ibid., p. 263.

8. Arnold Gingrich, *Nothing But People: The Early Days at Esquire, A Personal History, 1928–1958* (New York: Crown, 1971), p. 21.

9. John Mercer, *The Informational Film* (Champaign, Ill.: Stipes Publishing Company, 1981), p. 24.

10. *Educational Screen*, vol. XXXI, no. 9 (November 1952), p. 404.

11. Interview with the author, May 7, 1977.

12. *Educational Screen*, vol. XIV, no. 10 (December 1935), p. 294.

13. *Film News*, vol. VII, no. 3 (December 1945), p. 19.

14. Arthur Edwin Krows, "Motion Pictures—Not for Theatres," *Educational Screen*, vol. XVIII, no. 10 (December 1939), p. 364.

15. Quotes are taken from contemporary Castle Films catalogs.

16. For more information on Soundies, see Maurice Terenzio, Scott Mac-Gillivray, and Ted Okuda, *The Soundies Distributing Corporation of America: A History and Filmography* (Jefferson, N.C.: McFarland, 1991).

17. *Educational Screen*, vol. I, no. 1 (January 1922), p. 8.

18. *Business Screen*, vol. V, no. 4 (December 20, 1943), p. 30.

19. *Educational Screen*, vol. XXV, no. 1 (January 1946), p. 50.

20. John Grierson, "Non-Theatrical Revolution," *Film News*, vol. V, no. 9 (November 1944), pp. 4–5.

21. Amos Vogel, "Cinema 16 Explained," *Film News*, vol. VIII, no. 10 (March-April 1948), p. 19.

22. L. C. Larson, "The Formation of the Educational Film Library Association," *Film News*, vol. IV, no. 1 (Summer 1943), p. 11. Most of the information on EFLA's formation is taken from Larson's article.

23. Emily S. Jones, "Remembering EFLA: 1945–1958," *Sightlines*, vol. XVII, nos. 1/2 (Fall/Winter 1983/84), p. 7.

EIGHT

Decades of Progress
and Prosperity

Non-theatrical film production and distribution prospered and grew in
the 1950s and 1960s; the industry was totally oblivious to what the
introduction of the first practical videotape recorder by Ampex in 1956
was to mean to the medium within a few short years. For the 1950s at
least, videotape had relevance only to the television industry, and the
television industry was pertinent to the non-theatrical film industry only
as a further outlet for its productions.

Between 1949 and 1951 the number of non-theatrical film libraries
increased from 897 to 2,002, with the largest number (1,351) handling
educational films and the smallest (633) distributing religious-oriented
productions. The third largest group of libraries (134) was located in
Chicago and its environs; New York came second with 196 libraries; and
California led the field with 217. By 1953, the number of libraries had
increased to 2,660, again with the largest groups located in California
and New York. Of these libraries, 503 were operated by schools or by
public school systems.

The 1950s were dominated by two successful efforts to create festival
showplaces for non-theatrical films. The idea for a non-theatrical film
festival was not new. From October 11 to November 29, 1947, the Chicago Film Council held the First Films of the World Festival, described
as "a giant preview of 16mm films." The Cleveland Film Council was
organized in the fall of 1947 by a group of citizens interested in 16mm

technical and educational films. In June 1948 it organized its first film festival, at which ninety-nine productions were screened in the following categories: Sales Promotion and Public Relations, Safety and Fire Fighting, Employee Training, Mental Hygiene, Art and Music, Religion, Industrial Relations, Supervisory Training, Adult Education, Teaching and Classroom, and Travel. A similar film festival was held in Chicago in 1949 and in Boston in 1951.

In 1957, the Film Council of America held its last Golden Reel Festival, an annual event since the 1940s, which had showcased non-theatrical films and helped encourage their presentation in international festivals. Prior to the demise of the Golden Reel Festival, discussions had taken place as to the best means of evaluating non-theatrical films for placement in international festivals; and on October 24–25, 1957, a conference was held at the National Education Center in Washington, D.C., chaired by Stanley Mackintosh, director of education and community services with the Motion Picture Association of America. As a result of that meeting the Committee on International Nontheatrical Events (CINE) was created to serve as a central facility to provide information on film festivals abroad and to help American non-theatrical filmmakers enter their productions in such events. The first annual meeting of CINE was held in October 1958, but it was not until November 1963 that CINE was incorporated under the laws of the District of Columbia, with the name "Committee" being changed to "Council." That same year a permanent secretariat was established in Washington, D.C.

Juries appointed by CINE's board of directors view submitted films, selecting those most suitable to represent the United States in competitions abroad. All selected professional films receive a Golden Eagle certificate, while selected amateur and student films receive Eagle certificates. CINE's selection and placement of films at foreign festivals has come under increasing criticism from young, independent filmmakers who, with valid reason, consider CINE representative of the American filmmaking establishment and out of touch with any type of experimental filmmaking that differs from the norm and might be considered to present a critical view of the United States. As a result, CINE's influence has decreased in recent years, and most filmmakers have few problems in placing their films directly with international festivals. CINE has moved sufficiently with the times to open up its competition to video productions beginning in 1982.

Concurrent with the creation of CINE, the Educational Film Library Association decided to found its own film festival, the American Film Festival, first held in New York in April 1959. The idea had originated with Leo Dratfield in the summer of 1958, and the first festival was organized by EFLA's president Elliott Kone and administrative head Emily S. Jones. The American Film Festival made awards in a variety of subject categories, with the finalists selected by volunteer prescreening committees. By its third year, the festival was able to boast of more than 500 entries and more than 600 attendees.

With the retirement of Emily S. Jones, the American Film Festival established a new award in 1969, the "Emily," given to the film with the highest numerical rating of any film shown at the festival. The first winner was *Ski the Outer Limits*, produced by Summit Films, Inc. The American Film Festival remains the leading non-theatrical film event, with its only major competition coming with the creation of the Birmingham Educational Film Festival, first held from March 12–16, 1973. The festival was presented in conjunction with the Alabama Education Association and with financing from the Alabama Power Company. The first year some 250 films were entered in competition, with thirty-four finalists meeting the festival's criteria as "films which make original, creative and instructive contributions to the use of audio-visual media in the classroom."

Aside from the American Film Festival, EFLA's other major new activity was the creation of a new magazine, *Sightlines*, first published in May–June 1967. The name was chosen by James Limbacher, and initial editorial duties were undertaken by Emily S. Jones, who recalled:

> Editorial content was never a problem. We had a special theme for each issue, and dragooned members (usually Board members) into writing on the subject. Selecting cover illustrations was a new challenge, and we were always on the lookout for free photographs. Stills from new films were one good source; and for the summer American Film Festival issue, we could choose from a rich supply of photographs taken during screenings or at the Awards' ceremony.
>
> Advertising never came in as briskly as we had hoped. At that time, there were a large number of AV magazines, so advertisers spread their budgets around. For a while, we had an agent who was supposed to round up ads for us, but he was no more effective than the EFLA staff, and he took a commission. So the chore of selling ads was another task for the staff. But Sightlines was a success with its readers from the beginning.[1]

Sightlines was far from being the first of EFLA's publications; it produced a *Film Evaluation Guide*, *Film Review Digest*, *Service Supplements*, and a *Bulletin*, which was merged with *Sightlines* but revived in its own right in September 1977. A 1961 publication, *Films for Children*, proved reasonably successful. The person most associated with *Sightlines* is Judith Trojan, who was its managing editor from 1972 to 1982, its senior editor from 1982 to 1984, and its editor-in-chief from 1984 to 1988.

In 1957, non-theatrical filmmakers banded together to form the Industrial Film Producers Association, which later changed its name to the less limiting Informational Film Producers of America. With more than 1,200 members in 1978, it promoted itself as the largest organization of non-theatrical filmmakers, making annual CINDY awards in the categories of films, videotapes, film strips, and slide presentations and also promoting government contracts for its member producers.

On an international level the International Association of Informational Film Distributors was founded in Brussels in 1958 by Jan Botermans and G. F. Magnel. Created to distribute sponsored films on a worldwide basis, the association held its first meeting in 1960, attended by delegates from Belgium, the Netherlands, Switzerland, and the United Kingdom. The United States was not represented until a January 1961 meeting in Bern, Switzerland, attended by Frank Arlinghaus of Modern Talking Picture Service. That meeting drew up a series of rules and regulations and formalized the association.

To serve the needs of international producers of non-theatrical films, IQ, the International Quorum of Motion Picture Producers, was formed in 1966. The bulk of the membership—70 out of 140—was American, including Spottiswood Studios (Mobile, Alabama), Films for Information (Palo Alto, California), Paragon Productions (Oakton, Virginia), Sage Films (Helena, Montana), the Walter J. Klein Co. Ltd. (Charlotte, North Carolina), and Piccadilly Films International (San Antonio, Texas). One U.S. member was Pittsburgh-based The Latent Image, whose owner George A. Romero left industrial film production in 1968 to produce and direct the cult horror classic, *Night of the Living Dead*.

The worldwide production and distribution of non-theatrical films is a further indication of the industry's growth, and growth in any medium generally leads to outside interest and investment. The non-theatrical film industry held considerable appeal for the publishing community, in part because of the obvious parallels between the two. Both mediums inform and educate, and both are equally concerned with fulfilling needs as leisure activities.

The publishing industry's involvement with non-theatrical film began in earnest in 1940 with Coronet Productions (see chapter 7) and reached its zenith in the 1960s. Originally it was a logical interest, in that educational films could supplement published texts, but at the same time the acquisitions were influenced by the profit motive. According to Esquire-Coronet employee Arnold Gingrich, an attempted takeover of the company by another publishing house arose not out of a desire to acquire two popular periodicals but out of a desire for the concern's non-theatrical film activities: "The educational film division gave the company glamour in the eyes of investors at a time when publishing stocks were not fashionable. It was the Coronet Films that Crowell-Collier were after when they began the attempt at a raid on us, resulting in their doubling the price of our stock, from 13 to 26, in just one month."[2] Esquire-Coronet, Inc., did not survive as an independent company for too much longer; in the 1970s the entire operation, including periodicals and film division, was acquired by the New York publishing house of Simon & Schuster, and in 1984 it lost its identity with a merger into Gulf + Western Industries, Inc.

Following Coronet, the first major entry into the non-theatrical field by a publishing house came in 1946, when the McGraw-Hill Book Company announced plans to form an educational film division that would produce subjects supplemental to the company's textbooks. President James S. Thompson explained:

"The textbooks will continue as the basic source of information to be transferred to the student under the direction of the teacher. This transfer can be aided and hastened by motion pictures. . . . The function of motion pictures will be to dramatize and give realistic explanation of theories, principles, techniques, and applications. In addition, by means of animated drawings, photomicrography, and slow-motion photography, we can help the student to visualize what is normally difficult to see."[3]

The first four books to be filmed were *Engineering Drawing* by T. E. French, *Mechanical Drawing* by French and C. L. Svensen, *Textbook of Healthful Living* by H. S. Diel, and *Student Teaching* by R. Schorling. The McGraw-Hill Text Films Department was headed initially by Albert J. Rosenberg, who had formerly been aviation specialist with the U.S. Office of Education. McGraw-Hill further extended its operations in 1972 with the acquisition of Contemporary Films, a major non-theatrical distributor of foreign-language features and quality entertainment films.

Crowell, Collier and Macmillan was the most aggressive of publishing houses in the acquisition of non-theatrical assets. In 1967, it purchased the 16mm entertainment film rental company Audio Film Center, which had been founded in 1951 by Myron Bresnick as Fleetwood Films and named for the area of Mount Vernon in which Bresnick lived. (Bresnick had entered the industry in 1945 with Walter O. Gutlohn, and his company had acquired the last remaining assets of Ideal Pictures Corporation in 1967.) In 1968, Crowell, Collier and Macmillan purchased Brandon Films, another 16mm entertainment films distributor, founded in 1940 by Thomas (Tom) Brandon. The publisher merged Audio and Brandon under the new name of Macmillan-Audio-Brandon.

Thomas Brandon (1910–1982) was active in the 1930s helping distribute films advocating liberal and social issues; he co-founded with playwright Sidney Howard one of New York's first film societies, Film Forum, Inc. Writing in *The New Yorker* (May 20, 1974), Penelope Gilliatt called Brandon "the fine-faced man of the thirties who set out in 1931 with Lewis Jacobs to make a film on the exploitation of the blacks in Alabama, Tennessee, and Georgia." That film was never made, because Brandon's ultimate interest lay more in film distribution and exhibition than production. Through his efforts, many fine foreign films and non-Hollywood American films found audiences. As he explained to *Variety* (September 6, 1967), "You have to get people used to the idea of seeing great films of the past. There are many communities where the educated people simply have not had anything like this offered to them before. And I also feel that people will come and see offbeat new films if presented in a context of great old ones."

In the area of educational and industrial film, Crowell, Collier and Macmillan purchased Association Films in 1968. Originally a division of the YMCA, Association Films had been incorporated in 1949 as an independent entity, headed by A. L. Frederick and J. R. Bingham. The latter had joined the YMCA in 1911, and Frederick joined in 1917; they remained with the association until their retirements in, respectively, 1968 and 1967.

In 1970, Crowell, Collier and Macmillan acquired Sterling Movies, Inc., which had been formed in 1954 by Charles F. Dolan as the industrial film distribution division of Sterling Films, Inc. Sterling Films, Inc. was founded in 1946 by Saul J. Turell and Robert Rhoades as a producer and distributor of educational short subjects. Sterling Movies U.S.A. was purchased from the parent company in 1956 by Charles F. Dolan. In 1967, Sterling Movies U.S.A. began producing a newsreel format series titled Theatre Cavalcade, presenting industrial and business news to theatregoers.

Meredith Publishing Company, whose assets included *Better Homes and Gardens*, acquired an interest in the Princeton Film Center, Inc., in 1951. That educational film distributor, which has no relationship to the university, had been founded in 1940 by Gordon Knox.

Even the academic publishing field was not immune from interest in the non-theatrical film. In 1971, Greenwood Press produced an educational film titled *North from Mexico*, based on its then best-selling reprint of Cary McWilliams' book of the same title. Despite Greenwood's being very much not a film distributor, it was able to sell 400 copies of the film, through judicious advertising in *Film News* and elsewhere, and decided to distribute further titles from the film's producer, Sumner Glimsher, who had formerly been with the Center for Mass Communications at Columbia University Press.

Neither were the non-theatrical film's support activities exempt from takeovers by the publishing industry. In August 1968, Harcourt Brace & World, Inc., became associated with the publication of *Business Screen* through its acquisition of the Brookhill Division, Ojibway Press, Inc. The journal was subsequently sold to Back Stage Productions as of January 1977 and soon thereafter merged into the newspaper-style publication *Back Stage*.

Changes were also taking place in the very film stock on which non-

theatrical films were distributed. Polyester-base film, which is supposedly less likely to scratch in multiple use but was accused of damaging
projection equipment, was introduced in October 1969 by Eastman Kodak under the trade name of "Estar." The process was patented in 1950
by the British Imperial Chemical Industries (ICI), and the American
rights were acquired the following year by Du Pont. Four years later, it
began production of polyester-base film stock under the trade name of
"Cronar," signing a licensing agreement with Eastman Kodak in September 1955.[4]

The most important technical innovation in non-theatrical film since
the coming of sound took place in the 1960s with the introduction of
8mm film to the educational and industrial fields. Mark Slade, education
liaison officer of the National Film Board of Canada, hailed 8mm in 1962
as "the Eighth Lively Art," describing it as "a mass-transit system of
the senses."[5]

As a substandard, home-movie film gauge, 8mm had been around
since the early 1930s. Eastman Kodak introduced it in 1932 as a film
stock for the amateur movie-maker, far less expensive than 16mm (of
which, of course, it is half the width). Two years later, Bell & Howell
brought out its first 8mm projector, the Filmo 8, followed in 1935 by its
first 8mm camera, the Filmo Straight 8. Eastman Kodak introduced color
to 8mm in 1936 with "Kodachrome" film stock. In 1940, magazine load-
ing, which helped the user in handling the film, became a reality with
the Cine-Kodak camera.

Although 8mm was popular, there was no question that it was film
stock for the amateur. It had no professional recognition, except from a
handful of independent and avant-garde filmmakers, and was so narrow
that it was laughingly compared to a bootlace. However, two events in
the 1960s altered the way in which 8mm was viewed by the non-theatrical
film industry. In 1960, Fairchild Camera and Instrument Corporation introduced an 8mm sound camera and projector. The following year, it announced the "MoviePak," the first 8mm sound cartridge that could be
slotted into a cartridge projector, requiring no clumsy threading of the
film within the machine; it was, in theory at least, as simple to operate as
are today's videotape players. In 1962, Technicolor introduced its first
8mm silent cartridge projector.

The cartridge projector was a perfect means of presenting films in
settings as varied as the classroom and the salesroom. The basic advantage of the cartridge load projector was that it was foolproof. Coupled
with a rear-screen projection set-up, it could offer "instant" movies
without the need to darken a room. Within a short time a number of
other manufacturers, including Paillard, MPO Vidtronics, and Jayark,
brought out similar cartridge load projectors. Unfortunately the shortsighted manufacturers failed to make their individual systems compat-

ible with each other, which was eventually to be a contributing factor to the demise of 8mm cartridge load projectors and the rapid growth in the sale of videotape players.

The second 8mm innovation came in May 1965, when Eastman Kodak introduced Super 8mm, with a picture image supposedly equal to that of 16mm. Within a few short years, Super 8mm completely eclipsed Standard 8mm (as its predecessor came to be known) for home use and was adopted more and more often by professionals working with non-theatrical film. Super 8mm and the cartridge load projector were brought together in 1973, when Eastman Kodak perfected the Ektasound projector. (The popularity of Super 8mm also led to Eastman Kodak's introducing Super 16mm, which offered more picture area than regular 16mm, thus making it ideal for blow-up to 35mm. Of course, Super 16mm was primarily intended as a cheap alternative to 35mm in theatrical production and has little if any relevance to non-theatrical filmmaking.)

Cheap and easy to use, Super 8mm had by the early 1970s become extremely popular with professionals in the field, but the majority of releases in Super 8mm were, in reality, shot in 16mm and reduced in size. One of the first companies to begin professional production in Super 8mm was Sanri Super 8 Productions, founded in New York in 1970 by Henri Wolfe. The previous year, the Society of Motion Picture and Television Engineers had helped to promote the new format by hosting a two-day symposium, on October 2 and 3, on Super 8mm Film Production Techniques.

A major breakthrough in the use of Super 8mm came in September 1972, when the Chrysler Corporation supplied information together with sales and service training films (produced by Ross, Roy, Inc.) promoting the company's 1973 line of cars to its dealers in Super 8mm only. "The Super 8 sound movie is more than a different way of doing the same old thing. It is the beginning of a new concept in communications," commented *Business Screen* at the beginning of 1975.[6]

In theory the use of Super 8mm in production should have died out as quickly as the use of 8mm projectors with the growth of videotape; in practice, some producers have continued to use Super 8mm for filming and then immediately transfer the film to videotape for editing and ultimate presentation. This is particularly the procedure in the production of music videos, the medium that more than any other has helped to keep Super 8mm alive.

With both equipment and raw stock costing far less, 8mm was rapidly taking over from 16mm in the 1960s in both the home and the non-theatrical markets. As early as the summer of 1961, Eastman Kodak's John Flory had prophesied that "the growth of the use of 8mm sound film was greatly exceeding the rate of increase of 16mm usage."[7] As of 1965, *Business Screen* reported there were some five million 8mm projectors in use in the United States.[8] By 1971, there were almost as many manufacturers of 8mm projectors as of 16mm machines, thirteen compared to fifteen.

The educational use of 8mm sound films was the subject of a conference from November 8 to 10, 1961, sponsored by the Project in Educational Communication at Teachers College, Columbia University. Conference coordinator Professor Louis Forsdale argued, "In the largest sense the dream is that 8mm sound film can make motion pictures available everywhere—in the classrooms, libraries, homes—so that the great power of the medium as a teaching-learning tool can be released."[9] Robert Wagner, director of the Motion Picture Division at Ohio State University called 8mm sound film "a state of mind, with horizons as far in each direction as the most sophisticated cinema student at the one end, and the pre-school youngster at the other."[10]

In 1964, the Sixth American Film Festival presented four programs aimed at showing the best in 8mm, and in August of the same year, *Film News* introduced a new 8mm sound column, co-edited by Alan Rogers and Jim Witker. It was all very positive, but in retrospect many of the points made by academics and educators with regard to 8mm sound were no different than those made thirty or so years earlier when 16mm sound was introduced. In a retrograde step taking 8mm sound back to the early days of 16mm sound, Americom Corporation in 1965 introduced "Ameridisc," an 8mm sound-on-disc process. The company first marketed entertainment shorts and features in the process and tried to generate interest from the industrial and educational fields. Ameridisc died as quickly and as unmourned as 16mm sound-on-disc.

To satisfy the needs of owners of 8mm projectors, a number of companies began releasing 8mm versions of major Hollywood productions. One of the first studios to become involved in the field was Columbia Pictures, which established an 8mm division in the mid-1970s, releasing condensed (or as it described them "digest") versions of a number of its features, including *The Wild One* (1954), *The Guns of Navarone* (1961), *Lawrence of Arabia* (1962), and *Cat Ballou* (1965). Universal followed in 1979 with the creation of Universal 8 Films, which offered one- or two-reel condensations of *The Sting* (1973), *High Plains Drifter* (1973), *Jaws* (1975), *Slap Shot* (1977), *Smokey and the Bandit* (1977), *National Lampoon's Animal House* (1978), *Jaws 2* (1978), *Battlestar Galactica* (1978), *Dracula* (1979), and *Buck Rogers* (1979).

In 1976, New York–based Ivy Films (which was 16mm distributor for NTA, Inc., Republic Pictures, Inc., and M. & A. Alexander, Inc.) released a group of features available for sale or rental in their entirety in Super 8mm. Included were *The Third Man* (1950), *High Noon* (1952), *Road to Bali* (1952), *The Quiet Man* (1952), *Invasion of the Body Snatchers* (1952), and *Animal Farm* (1955). In 1980, a New York company named Marketing Film International began selling a group of Paramount features on Super

8mm, available in digest (one reel), select scenes (three reels), and complete versions. Among the first releases were *War of the Worlds* (1953), *To Catch a Thief* (1955), *The Godfather* (1972), *Saturday Night Fever* (1977), *Grease* (1978), and *Star Trek—the Motion Picture* (1979).

Most 8mm users were awaiting M-G-M's entry into the field, but when the studio finally decided to release a batch of twelve of its features in 1977 they were in the form of twenty-minute condensations rather than complete features. The first twelve titles to be available were *Mutiny on the Bounty* (1935), *The Wizard of Oz* (1939), *Easter Parade* (1948), *The Barkleys of Broadway* (1948), *Battleground* (1949), *Quo Vadis?* (1951), *An American in Paris* (1951), *Ivanhoe* (1952), *How the West Was Won* (1962), *Doctor Zhivago* (1965), *Shaft* (1971), and *Logan's Run* (1976). Six Tom and Jerry cartoons were also made available, and an additional twelve features were promised for the following year. The films were marketed under the M-G-M Super–8mm banner and distributed by Ken Films.

The 1970s and early 1980s were the heyday for those who collected films on 8mm and 16mm. Dozens of companies sprang up offering films for sale on one or the other or both gauges at affordable prices. The films available for sale were generally in the public domain and the print quality varied considerably from dealer to dealer, but the market was lucrative for both buyer and seller. Among the companies specializing in 8mm sales were Cinema Eight (in Chester, Connecticut) and Milestone Movies Corporation (in Monroe, Connecticut). Companies that sold 16mm public domain films, all of which are now defunct, include Canterbury Films (in Great Neck, New York), Ed Finney (in Los Angeles), Mizzell Films (in Pasadena), and Storace Films (in Scottsdale, Arizona). A few of the companies selling 16mm films in the 1970s have survived through to the 1990s, generally by expanding into the video field: Encore Entertainment (in Anaheim, California), Glenn Photo Supply (in Encino, California), Griggs-Moviedrome (in Nutley, New Jersey), National Cinema Service (in Ho-Ho-Kus, New Jersey), and Reel Images (in Botsford, Connecticut).

Even the haughty Film Department of the Museum of Modern Art recognized the need to make available 16mm prints of a limited number of their holdings for collectors and others to own. (Since the late 1930s, the museum had been distributing films to selected institutions and by 1941 reported that it had circulated ninety-one programs from its collection to 476 institutions.) In 1979, Bob Summers, then head of the museum's film circulation program, initiated a program of leasing selected 16mm films to individuals and organizations for the life of the prints. The average price of a film was $45 per reel, and among the first releases were *Broken Blossoms* (1919), *Fall of Troy* (1910), *Germany Awake!* (1968), *Hearts of the World* (1918), *The Land* (1942), *The Martyrs of the Alamo*

(1915), *The Plow That Broke the Plains* (1936), *St. Louis Blues* (1929), and *War Comes to America* (1945).

The one company that dominated the area of 8mm and 16mm sales, in terms of both the quantity and the quality of its materials, was Blackhawk Films, founded by Kent D. Eastin (1909–1981). Fascinated by films as a child, Eastin founded his company at his parent's home in Galesburg, Illinois, in 1927. He would purchase large quantities of 16mm films from companies that had either lost the rights or entered bankruptcy and then resell the films to collectors. It proved a remarkably profitable venture, and by the mid-1930s Eastin was promoting his company, then known as Eastin Entertainment Films, as a major supplier of 16mm subjects.

In 1935, Eastin moved to Davenport, Iowa; he renamed his company Blackhawk Films in 1939 after the Indian tribe that had once owned the land on which the city was built. In 1947, Martin Phelan became Eastin's partner, and the holding company became Eastin-Phelan Corporation. Blackhawk's expansion began in earnest in the 1950s, when Eastin, who was a dedicated railroad buff, began releasing various railroad subjects in 8mm. Blackhawk was able to negotiate non-theatrical rights to the various Hal Roach–produced shorts featuring Laurel and Hardy, Our Gang, Charley Chase, and others. A similar contract was signed with 20th Century-Fox, granting Blackhawk limited rights to the Fox Movietone newsreels and to various shorts, including *Broadway by Day* (1930) and *Mississippi Showboat* (1931). From Paul Killiam in New York, Blackhawk acquired non-theatrical rights to the television series *Movie Museum* and *Silents Please*, which had been compiled from silent features and shorts, together with a number of silent features owned by Killiam.

Under Kent Eastin's benevolent guidance, Blackhawk also worked with the American Film Institute, helping to fund the acquisition and preservation of various titles in return for access to the films for 8mm and 16mm release. In 1975, David Shepard, who had come to Blackhawk from the American Film Institute, was able to negotiate an arrangement with the Museum of Modern Art, whereby Blackhawk helped restore a number of D. W. Griffith–directed Biograph shorts, in return for which Blackhawk was again able to offer the titles for sale in 8mm and 16mm.

Although 16mm had been the mainstay of Blackhawk for the first three decades of its life, it was 8mm that proved the more profitable in the 1970s and 1980s. David Shepard explained, "All the 16mm activity taken together was less than 20% of the business and most of that was public library sales. The 80% of the business—and we're talking dollar volume, not unit volume—was in 8mm prints that were being sold to individuals who enjoyed them as home movies. And also they had 8mm collections placed in about 1500 public libraries at one time."[11]

Something unique about Blackhawk releases were the introductory historical titles. Sometimes they were one or two title cards long, and sometimes as many as six or seven. In the early years, the authors were never identified; but later one discovered that among those responsible for providing the historical data were Edward Wagenknecht, Kalton Lahue, and even Anthony Slide. This writer still cringes when he sees one of those films with his introduction being screened, but at the same time marvels that he managed to be so noncommittal and inconsequential about a film he detested or that, as in the case of *The Juggernaut*, he managed to find a supposedly satisfactory reason that Blackhawk was releasing only the last reel of a five-reel feature.

In 1975, Blackhawk Films was acquired by Lee Enterprises, a newspaper and television conglomerate with headquarters in Davenport, Iowa. Two years later, Lee also purchased the film buff/collector monthly newspaper *Classic Images*. Perhaps because of its size, Lee Enterprises was not successful in its management of the company and soon resold it to a group of Blackhawk executives. The company's finances continued to suffer, largely because videotape sales were cutting heavily into 8mm and 16mm sales. In the mid-1980s, Blackhawk was sold for a third time, to Republic Pictures, which closed down the Davenport facility and moved the company to Los Angeles, where it was transformed into an exclusively video operation. In 1989, the film assets of the company were acquired by David Shepard, who currently markets the Blackhawk films, in 16mm only, through his company Film Preservation Associates.

In the area of 16mm film rental libraries, the major force was Films Inc. The company was acquired in 1968 by Public Media, Inc., which was owned by Charles Benton (b. 1931). The son of William Benton, Charles had been involved in production at Encyclopaedia Britannica Films from 1953 to 1955 and worked as an administrative assistant at Films Inc. from 1959 to 1960. When he acquired Films Inc., the company controlled 16mm non-theatrical rights to the releases of three major Hollywood studios, Paramount, Metro-Goldwyn-Mayer, and 20th Century-Fox. Benton hired a work force of young, enthusiastic executives and worked both to enhance and consolidate Films Inc.'s position. In 1971, he formed the first 16mm public library division at the company and created a college marketing division, Campus Entertainment Network. Then 16mm rights to additional producers and studios were added, including ABC Motion Pictures, New World, First Artists, Orion, pre-1948 RKO titles, American Film Theatre productions, the feature films of Charlie Chaplin, Embassy, American-International, and Columbia.

In time, two other 16mm houses, Janus Film and Macmillan-Audio-Brandon, were added to Films Inc.'s very substantial library. A slew of catalogs indicate the scope of the company's activities: *The Whole Library*

Catalog, General Entertainment Catalog (listing 1,600 features), *The Expanded Cinema Catalog*, the *Educational Catalog, Feature Films for Lease, Foreign Films Catalog*, and *The Irresistible Silver Screen Komic Katalog*. The second edition of the Films Inc., catalog *Rediscovering the American Cinema*, edited in 1977 by Doug Lemza, was hailed as a valuable text on the history of American film. It was, in reality, nothing more than a partial catalog of Films Inc.'s holdings, but those holdings were so substantial that a listing of them read like a catalog of America's major film productions.

Films Inc., tried to expand more into the educational field in 1977, when it began marketing MovieStrips, which told the story of selected feature films through approximately 400 frames and accompanying audio tape(s). A selection of titles from M-G-M were offered at $49.50 each.

In 1979, Films Inc., entered theatrical distribution, opening a New York office headed by Tom Bernard and acquiring U.S. theatrical and non-theatrical rights to Jerzy Skolimowski's *The Shout*. Further expanding into the theatrical field, the company embarked on a new venture with Quartet Films (founded in 1977) in 1979, creating a new company Quartet/Films Inc., which would acquire productions for both theatrical and non-theatrical release. In 1986, Films Inc., entered theatrical exhibition, taking over operation of the Film Forum 2 theatre in New York.

The 1970s and early 1980s were the "golden years" for Films Inc.—it grossed $30 million in 1983—and for other 16mm rental libraries. The number of such libraries is substantial, with the majority having 100 or so titles and operating often on a part-time basis. Both the larger and the small libraries were scattered throughout the United States: The Film Center (in Washington, D.C.) maintained a varied library of public domain titles; Hurlock Cine World (Old Greenwich, Connecticut) handled releases from Allied Artists and Monogram; Modern Sound Pictures, Inc. (Omaha, Nebraska) operated a library of predominantly foreign-language titles but also controlled the right to Cecil B. DeMille's *The King of Kings* (1927) and a number of silent features produced by DeMille; Select Films (New York) distributed English and foreign-language releases; Swank Motion Pictures, Inc. (St. Louis), was the major 16mm distributor for Universal; Westcoast Films (San Francisco) had a library primarily of public domain titles; and Clem Williams Films (Pittsburgh) distributed a number of Disney, Universal, and Paramount releases.

Some companies enjoyed the benefit of having been in existence for decades. Roa's Films in Milwaukee, which remained active through the 1980s as a 16mm library of reasonably priced public domain features and industrial, religious, and educational subjects, was an outgrowth of Photoart Visual Service, founded by Mrs. Roa Kraft Birch in 1926 as a photographic equipment supplier. Mrs. Birch disposed of her interest in the company in 1955. Twyman Films, Inc. (Dayton, Ohio), took over the distribution of the films claimed to be owned by infamous film entrepreneur Raymond Rohauer from Macmillan-Audio-Brandon. Through various questionable methods, Rohauer had obtained "rights" to a variety of films generally considered to be in the public domain, including features of Buster Keaton, Douglas Fairbanks, Harry Langdon, D. W. Griffith, and Mack Sennett. In the late 1980s, Twyman's owner Alan Twyman disposed of his interest in the company and distributed the Raymond Rohauer titles on a personal basis, using the company name "Alan Twyman Presents" until his death in 1990.

One manner in which public domain 16mm rental houses could win an advantage over competitors was by offering the highest quality prints detailed in well-produced, informative catalogs. The company that best illustrates this method is Radim/Film Images, founded in Chicago in the 1970s by a former Brandon Films employee, Art Brown.

Many 16mm rental houses specialized in foreign language and/or quality English-language titles. The best known of this group, all with offices in New York, were Almi Cinema, Corinth Films, New Line Cinema, and New Yorker Films. Independent and avant-garde filmmakers, such as Kenneth Anger, Stan Brakhage, Jonas Mekas, and Stan Vanderbeek, distributed their productions through Canyon Cinema Cooperative in San Francisco and Film-Makers Cooperative in New York. There was some limited highly specialized distribution, with Arthur Cantor, Inc., in New York distributing films on the arts, music, and theatre and Warren Miller in Southern California offering ski movies for rental and sale. Miller cleverly promoted his self-produced films with the suggestion that purchasers splice them into their own amateur efforts, to "fool your friends" and "liven up your home movies."

All of the 16mm rental libraries discussed in this chapter flourished in the 1970s and 1980s, evidence of what appeared to be an ever-growing interest in the non-theatrical film. Within one decade only three—Films Inc., the Museum of Modern Art, and Swank—were still operational. As far as most people with an interest in the non-theatrical film were concerned, they were largely irrelevant.

NOTES

1. Emily S. Jones, "In the Beginning: Sightlines," *Sightlines*, vol. XX, no. 2 (Winter 1986/87), p. 4.

2. Arnold Gingrich, *Nothing But the People: The Early Days at Esquire, A Personal History, 1928–1958* (New York: Crown, 1971), p. 169.

3. *Schools and Society*, vol. LXIV, no. 1667 (December 7, 1946), p. 398.

4. For more information, see Harriet Lundgaard, "The Case for Polyester Base," *Sightlines*, vol. XV, no. 4 (Summer 1982), pp. 14–16.

5. Mark Slade, "Eight Millimeter: The Eighth Lively Art," *Educational Screen & Audio-Visual Guide*, vol. XXXXI, no. 10 (July-October 1962), p. 598.

6. Jeorg Agin, "Super 8 Stronger Than Ever," *Business Screen*, vol. XXXVI, no. 1 (January/February 1975), p. 30.

7. John Flory, "The Challenge of 8mm Sound Film," *Educational Screen & Audio-Visual Guide*, vol. XXXX, no. 7 (July 1961), p. 334.

8. *Business Screen*, vol. XXV, no. 8 (January 1965), p. 41.

9. "Conference on 8mm Sound Film and Education," *Film News*, vol. XIX, no. 1 (January-February 1962), p. 6.

10. Ibid., p. 15.

11. Livio Jacob and Russell Merritt, "The Night I Saw Traffic in Souls: An Interview with David Shepard," *Griffithiana*, no. 38/39 (October 1990), p. 229.

NINE

The Waning Years

Videotape was on the brink of revolutionizing the non-theatrical field in the 1970s, but most in the industry seemed unaware of any potential change on the horizon. *Hope Reports*, which provided annual information on the financial status of the audiovisual industry, indicated no downward trend in industry's use of the medium. In 1973 alone, some $612 million was spent by American industry on the purchase of audiovisual materials and equipment. Educational production and distribution in the early 1970s continued to be dominated by Coronet and Encyclopaedia Britannica Films. There had been two new entrants in the field, Pyramid Films, founded in 1960 by David Adams, and Churchill Films, founded the following year by Robert (Bob) Churchill; to a large extent they were to lead the way in defining the new non-theatrical movement.

Pyramid Films was created originally to handle emergency medical films, but quickly it made a name for itself in the distribution of quality documentaries. Churchill handled social documentaries. Both companies understood that to survive they had to expand into the business and health film markets and would need actively to embrace video.

Lee Burdett, vice president of marketing for Encyclopaedia Britannica, opined that "the biggest changes in our business in the 1960s were the growth in competition caused by the many new companies and the growth in the marketplace caused by the regionalization and centralization of the buying agencies."[1] The quote typifies the attitudes of the older non-theatrical leaders. They saw the genre inexorably tied to business and industry. They ignored the tremendous social pressures and eventual change that swept over the United States in the 1960s. On the home front and in the non-theatrical film, it was no longer business as usual. The Civil Rights movement and domestic opposition to the escalating war in Vietnam were far more influential than any sponsored film could hope to be. Industrial, business, and educational films were rapidly falling out of step with American society. A film on "How To Date" had no relevance to American schoolchildren facing the draft and deployment in Vietnam. A group of Caucasian actors demonstrating how to sell a product or operate machinery was increasingly offensive to an increasingly militant black work force.

A new breed of 16mm filmmaker was coming to the fore in the 1960s and 1970s, documenting subjects in a fashion that would have been considered if not anti-American at least unprofessional a few years earlier. Their films were not made for Coronet or Encyclopaedia Britannica and a captive school audience. They were advocating social change, and their audiences were an increasingly militant and constantly growing American minority in its teens and early twenties. Vietnam was perhaps the most popular of subjects, covered in 16mm documentaries such as Emile de Antonio's *In the Year of the Pig* (1969), Peter Davis' *The Selling of the Pentagon* (1971), and the Academy Award–winning feature from Peter Davis and Bert Schneider, *Hearts and Minds* (1975). The bleakest aspect of America's immediate past, the Army-McCarthy hearings, were scrutinized in Emile de Antonio's *Point of Order* (1964). Blacklisting was the subject of David Helpern, Jr.'s *Hollywood on Trial* (1976). Liberals who had labored for years in darkness were brought into the spotlight, as in Jerry Buck, Jr.'s *I. F. Stone's Weekly* (1973); and homosexuals were invited to leave their closets in Peter Adair's *Word Is Out: Stories of Some of Our Lives* (1978). The rights of organized labor were examined, as in Barbara Kopple's documentary on the activities of the United Mine Workers of America, *Harlan County USA* (1976).

The 16mm filmmaker most influential for bringing about change is Frederick Wiseman (b. 1930), a former Boston lawyer and professor of criminal law who perfected a style of filmmaking that he called "reality fiction," whereby he photographs the reality of a situation but edits the raw footage to present his own viewpoint. Sometimes called *cinema verité* or direct cinema, this style of filmmaking grew out of the availability in the 1960s and after of lightweight 16mm cameras and sound equipment. It was pioneered in the United States by Richard Leacock, Donn A. Pennebaker, the brothers Albert and David Maysles, and others and is generally dated from the 1960 Robert Drew–Richard Leacock documentary *Primary*.

Between 1967 and 1988, Wiseman produced nineteen feature-length documentaries, beginning with *Titicut Follies*. A film of a prison hospital for the mentally ill at the Massachusetts Institution at Bridgewater, *Titicut Follies* created considerable controversy for its frank documentation of the abuse of aging mentally retarded patients; the Commonwealth of Massachusetts took Wiseman to court to prevent the film's being shown and as a result, *Titicut Follies'* exhibition was for many severely limited.

Wiseman's films generally deal with established areas of American life, such as *High School* (1968), *Hospital* (1970), *Welfare* (1975), and *Racetrack* (1985). He profiled *Law and Order* with the Kansas City police department in 1969, Neiman-Marcus in *The Store* (1983), and the Strategic Air Command in *Missile* (1988). Reviewing *High School*, the distinguished critic Pauline Kael called Wiseman "probably the most sophisticated intelligence to enter the documentary field in recent years."

In order to distribute his film, Wiseman did not contract, as had been the normal practice in the past, with an established distributor but instead launched his own company, Zipporah Films, Inc. Other filmmakers were to follow suit. In 1972, New Day Films was founded as a cooperative of independent filmmakers distributing their films advocating social change. Among its releases in 16mm film and video were Lorraine Gray's *With Babies and Banners*, Amalie Rothschild's *Conversations with Willard Van Dyke*, and Joyce Chopra and Claudia Weill's *Joyce at 34*. New Day's original emphasis was on feminist filmmaking, but that changed even though the majority of the filmmakers involved were women, including Julia Reichert, Amalie Rothschild, and Claudia Weill.

In line with a new sophistication in 16mm production, distributors of 16mm entertainment subjects were becoming equally sophisticated in the marketing of their releases. The major venues for 16mm releases were college campuses, where screenings of 16mm features often brought their distributors into direct competition with local movie houses and theatrical distributors. Most college film societies screened 16mm features with no or negligible admission charges, while neighborhood theatres were charging two or three dollars for films of much the same vintage. Non-theatrical distributors denied charges of unfair competition, with Al Green, sales vice president at Films Inc., claiming, "Our experience has been that college showings actually help theatre business by stimulating general film interest."[2]

Even the theatrical pornographic film industry found non-theatrical markets for its product opening up on college campuses. The New York–based company S.R.O. Entertainment distributed 16mm versions of such popular porno items as *Deep Throat* and *The Devil in Miss Jones*; and *Oui* (December 1975) reported that Princeton, Cornell, Rutgers, and Yale Law School were among the colleges booking such features.

In an effort to safeguard their interests, eighteen companies involved in non-theatrical distribution of feature films banded together to form the Non-Theatrical Film Distributors Association, Inc. It was yet another in a long line of similar self-interest non-theatrical organizations, and it was as short-lived and relatively ineffective as all those that had gone before, although the reason may have been a dying market rather than a lack of resolve.

The 16mm entertainment industry had come a long way since the 1930s. Filmosound Library's general manager William F. Kruse recalled,

> Neither industry nor education had then heard much about 16mm. The inevitable response to a statement about 16mm film was, "what's *that?*" But here and there someone had heard of the new medium. Little by little a small coterie of distributors and users developed. These were regarded, however, as the "disreputables" in the motion picture industry, the low men on the totem pole. They were the gypsies of film; the pedlars; the roadshowmen who, with whatever pictures they were able to acquire and reduce from 35mm, beat the bushes in the boondocks of the country where people had never before seen a movie of any kind.
>
> In the cold of winter these folks came from miles around—on foot, in horse-drawn sleds and Model T Fords—through snow and sleet to the movie show in the village hall. In the heat of summer the show was in the town park or in an open field—long before the drive-in theater was invented (or shall we say it was invented by the early roadshowmen?). Nobody ever knew how many there were of these roadshowmen, but there were at least several hundred, from all indications; and what a job these fellows did for the motion picture! If ever anyone developed an audience, it was the rugged roadshowman, unheralded and unsung.[3]

The increasing popularity of videotape in the late 1970s led to a fast decline in the number of 16mm rental houses. Only a handful, led by Films Inc., were able to survive, and even that company was forced to close down all its regional offices, consolidating activities in Chicago. As more and more entertainment features became available on videotape and later on videodisc, there was less and less interest in renting the same titles in 16mm, whose prices simply were not compatible with those of video. A videotape or videodisc could be rented for between one and four dollars a night, while the same title in 16mm rented for $150 or higher. Even the rental charges asked for minor or public domain features of between $20 and $50 could not compete with video. Institutional users such as college film societies, hospitals, and senior citizen groups continued to rent 16mm titles because the films were projected on a big screen rather than viewed on a small television monitor, but even these groups were lost to the 16mm market as projection video was introduced. The lack of quality in the latter compared to 16mm projection was considered irrelevant from an economic viewpoint.

The situation was further exacerbated by the Eastman Kodak Company, which in an ever-continuing effort to make a profit in an ever-dwindling marketplace continued to increase the cost of 16mm raw stock. In the early 1970s, companies specializing in the sale of 16mm titles could offer their films at as little as $25 a reel. Twenty years later, in order to make a profit, the same establishments were charging as high as $100 per reel.

Purchasers of documentary and educational subjects were unable to understand why purchase prices needed to be so high, and their attitude spread over into the area of videotapes of non-theatrical titles offered for sale. Manufacturing costs for producing limited numbers of videotapes are high; and in order to meet both laboratory costs and production costs, non-theatrical videotape distributors were charging $200 or more for a thirty-minute production. From an economic standpoint, the price was justifiable. To the buyer, who was able to purchase videotapes of Hollywood feature films for as little as $19.95, the price was not.

Lee Burdett of Encyclopaedia Britannica tried to explain, "There simply is not enough potential volume in educational media to support $49 videos. We, and other nontheatrical distributors, must hold to a pricing structure that has existed since we've existed."[4]

A related problem was brought up at the same time by Bob Glore, vice president of Churchill Films: "Each video is sold about 30 percent lower in price than a corresponding 16mm film. In addition, ten or 15 years ago, a volume buyer might purchase numerous 16mm prints; today, that same buyer is much more likely to seek duplication rights—and at a pittance. But while income per unit is decreasing, distribution costs—production, promotion, and overhead such as rent, salaries, and supplies—are increasing, or at best remaining the same. It doesn't take a marketing genius to realize that when margins drop, volume must increase to make up the difference."[5]

The reference to duplication rights brings up an added problem with videotape releases, the simplicity for the purchaser of copying the tapes. Copyright might well put that purchaser on the wrong side of the law, but it is generally not an issue to an individual deciding to duplicate a videotape for a friend or colleague. Film piracy was, of course, an issue with 16mm rentals and sales, but it was never so simple for the casual user to duplicate a 16mm print, and many laboratories would refuse to handle such work unless they were assured there was no copyright violation.

The 16mm non-theatrical industry helped support many dozens of film laboratories nationwide. The 1949–50 edition of *Film World 16mm Film and Industry Directory* lists eighty-six film laboratories handling 16mm, many of them associated with non-theatrical production houses. As of 1991, in Los Angeles only five major laboratories are capable of printing and processing 16mm film—DeLuxe, Film Technology, Foto-Kem, Image Transform, and Yale—and only two of those routinely handle reduction from 35mm to 16mm. Additional problems face producers and distributors working with 16mm black-and-white film, which many laboratories do not want to handle.

Videotape's supplemental arm, television, ultimately proved damaging to the non-theatrical film. At first it had been welcomed as an additional medium for the presentation of sponsored films. The Broadcast Information Bureau, which documents the various types of programming available to television stations, published the *Free Film Source Book*, which in the 1970s listed more than 9,000 sponsored films available for free use on television. With cable television increasing its hold on the viewing public, there was an even bigger demand and audience for sponsored films.

The problem ultimately was that sponsors quickly realized that television could offer a far greater audience for their messages or products than any number of non-theatrical screenings. There was little point in sponsoring a non-theatrical film when a television commercial could reach a far wider audience. Further, television was killing the audience for business and educational films, as many independent television stations and the smaller cable networks presented saturation airings of such films. Audiences were turned off, and television executives turned against sponsored films, not accepting that it was overpresentation rather than the films themselves to which viewers were objecting.

Purists continued to argue against videotape, maintaining that it was not the manner in which films were meant to be seen. But then, as far as 35mm theatrical films are concerned, neither is 8mm or 16mm. With 16mm non-theatrical releases, production values were seldom high enough for anyone to care in which medium they were eventually viewed.

The declining fortunes of the non-theatrical film had a decisive impact on the Educational Film Library Association. Effective September 15, 1987, it changed its name to the American Film & Video Association and two months later moved from New York to less expensive accommodation in La Grange Park, a suburb of Chicago. The previous year, the association's American Film Festival had acknowledged the change in the status quo and selected the new name of American Film & Video Festival. None of the New York staff made the move to Illinois except executive director Ron MacIntyre. Primarily responsible for overseeing the changes, MacIntyre had been appointed executive director in March 1987, replacing Marilyn Levin, who resigned the previous November. MacIntyre remained as the association's administrative head until 1990.

The year after its move, the American Film & Video Association announced the establishment of the Leo Awards, created by the Leo Dratfield Endowment "to stimulate interest in independent and nontheatrical film and video and to support worthwhile film and video projects through awards, scholarships and special events." Two awards were to be presented annually to individuals "who show a sustained ability to introduce innovative and unorthodox approaches into their areas of specialization."[6] Despite such intent, the first two awards were more inclined toward recognition of the establishment in the non-theatrical field, going to EFLA's long-time administrative head Emily S. Jones and to the founder of Churchill Films, Robert (Bob) Churchill.

The Leo Awards were named for Leo Dratfield (1918–1986), who was a familiar figure at any and all film festivals remotely connected with non-theatrical or independent filmmaking. His first involvement with film came during the Second World War when he worked for the Office of War Information in New York and helped set up mobile film units for American troops during the North African campaign. In 1951, Englishman Charles Cooper was deported, a victim of the anti-Communist McCarthy-era witchhunts, and forced to sell his New York–based 16mm distribution company, Contemporary Films. (Cooper established a new Contemporary Films in London, which soon became a major distributor, in both 16mm and 35mm, of the best of world cinema.) With his partners James Britton and Rudy Kamerling, Leo Dratfield purchased Cooper's American company and acquired the U.S. rights to many important foreign-language films while providing a distribution outlet for the finest young American filmmakers. Contemporary Films was sold to McGraw-Hill in 1972, and Dratfield left the company the following year. He helped to establish Phoenix Films and worked at Films Inc., founding and editing a newsletter titled Kaleidoscope.

It is often the case that the decline of a medium leads to its discovery and acclaim by the academic community. In a small and limited way so it was with the non-theatrical film when, in 1975, the American Archives of the Factual Film was established at Iowa State University. The archives had their origins in a decision by Ott Coelln, the retired editor and publisher of *Business Screen*, to deposit his papers at the university. The archives was initially a part of the university library's Department of Special Collections and, as its curator Stanley Yates wrote,

> From the very beginnings there were heated and extended discussions on what to call this archive. Some objected to the use of "factual" because many films were simply propagandistic and/or dramatizations. Others complained that the term "non-theatrical" was too negative. Even the word "American" caused some consternation; did it mean films about America or simply that the archive was located in America? Whatever the arguments and counter arguments, it remains The American Archives of the Factual Film with all the unresolved ambiguities. . . .
>
> From the earliest days, the AAFF has been thought of as a research

depository. Films would not be loaned and copies would be made only upon receipt of permission to do so from the copyright holder. Still, the Archives continues to get requests which are stock footage in nature; within our limitations, we try to help. But the main thrust is research, research which usually entails prolonged use of our moviolas, looking at large numbers of films to gather information to answer research questions and to raise new ones. We feel that the AAFF offers unparalleled resources for research, limited only by the persistence, imagination and acuity of the researcher.[7]

One academic who has made use of the archives is Daniel J. Perkins, who is professor of telecommunications at the University of Wisconsin at Eau Claire and a consultant to the archives. He is one of the few and the first in the academic community to study non-theatrical film as a serious subject, writing as early as 1982 on the sponsored film as "a new dimension in American film research."[8] That essay noted some of the holdings of the American Archives of the Factual Film, and in so doing it helped provide a general idea of the number of films sponsored by some of the leading American industries active in the field:

> Sixty films from AT&T produced between 1947 and 1952.
>
> Forty films from the International Harvester Company produced between 1911 and 1971.
>
> Fifty films from the American Dental Association produced between 1945 and 1973.
>
> Seventy films from Smith, Kline and French produced between 1955 and 1977.
>
> One hundred fifty four films from the Union Pacific Railroad produced between 1941 and 1975.

These are only a few of the more than 23,000 cans of films in the collection, which is in urgent need of a major preservation, an effort hampered in large part by the lack of glamor associated with non-theatrical films. What individual or foundation wants to provide funding for, say, the Apex Film Corporation's 1951 production of *The Du Pont Story*, when the same money could be utilized to preserve a starring vehicle of Cary Grant, Spencer Tracy, or Jean Harlow?

The change of attitude toward non-theatrical films was also evident elsewhere. Educational films of the 1950s that had dealt with such matters as personal hygiene, dating, how to survive an atomic bomb explosion, how to use the library, or rudimentary sex education were now considered items of fun and humor. Morality and America's attitude toward it had changed drastically between the 1950s and the 1970s. The failure of many producers of educational films to copyright their works allowed other filmmakers to exploit them, often with humorous results. Educational and industrial films were now called "found footage," a continuing source of inspiration to the documentary and independent filmmaker.

In 1970, experimental filmmaker Standish Lawder produced *Dangling Participle*, in which he re-edited clips from a handful of 1950s sex-education short subjects in order to create a new short subject that has been described as the funniest American underground film. In Lawder's work what was once informational becomes antisexual and banal.

Another film that made new use of educational films, along with government-produced propaganda, was *The Atomic Cafe*, an eighty-eight-minute feature produced and directed by Pierce Rafferty, Jayne Loader, and Kevin Rafferty for The Archives Project, Inc., and released in 1982 after a reported seven years in production. *The Atomic Cafe* was a documentary compilation, without narration, of films dealing with the threat of nuclear war, including 1950s educational subjects of the "duck and cover" variety. It was received with mixed reviews. Writing in *New York* magazine (May 3, 1982), David Denby called *The Atomic Cafe* "a carnival of folly, a pop-culture distorting mirror of the nuclear age," while David Ansen in *Newsweek* (June 28, 1982) felt "it leaves you hungry for hard information: you don't learn anything, except how foolish we all were back in those malignantly innocent days." At the time it was considered quite unusual to produce a feature entirely comprised of archival footage, and *The Atomic Cafe* was indicative of the future for reuse of non-theatrical subjects of earlier decades.

Because producers had made educational and industrial films for sponsors, they had generally been lax either in copyrighting or in renewing the rights to such productions. As a result, a minor industry has developed in the exploitation of these films for other purposes. Stock footage libraries such as Patrick Montgomery's Archive Productions and Pierce Rafferty's Petrified Films (both located in New York) have sizeable libraries of educational and industrial films that they license as "stock footage" for use in anything and everything from films or videos used in training seminars to television commercials. The largest privately owned collection of educational and industrial films is that of Rick Prelinger, whose New York–based Prelinger Associates, Inc., has sizeable holdings of the productions of Audio Productions, Calvin, Caravel Films, Coronet, Encyclopaedia Britannica Films, Frith Films, the Jam Handy Organization, Jerry Fairbanks Productions, the William Matthews Company, McGraw-Hill, Mode-Art Pictures, Wilding Picture Productions, Young America, and many others.

Companies such as Prelinger have been able to find and exploit one new area of non-theatrical production, the corporate video. In general, it was prohibitively expensive to create 16mm productions not intended for widespread use but for presentation to, say, a company's share-holders or board of directors or for one-time screening to employees. The cheapness of videotape production—where the highest cost is in editing and photography is inexpensive and immediately changeable—has meant that one-time presentations, so-called corporate videos, have increased in popularity. Further, because a videotape of a corporate official explaining policy or practice can be both boring and uninformative, producers have turned more and more to stock footage, taking sequences from industrial or educational films, particularly from the 1950s, and turning them to comic effect.

The licensing of films for use as stock footage rather than for non-theatrical rentals has helped some 16mm libraries survive. With more than 10,000 titles, Los Angeles–based Budget Films continues as a major 16mm resource, founded under another name in 1950 by Al Dreben. The library includes releases from Columbia Pictures, Republic Picture, various independent productions, and a vast quantity of public domain titles, "clips" from which can be licensed for all manner of uses: in documentaries, television commercials, and even new feature films.

Since the 1970s, Budget Films has been able to change its priorities. It offers stock footage and ½" Heaven, a division providing videotapes for rental by mail with offerings based on the best of Budget's 16mm library. The number of employees has been halved—down to five full-time and three part-time in 1991—and 16mm rentals now make up only 30 percent of the company's business. In fact, the 16mm rentals are offered primarily as a public service to institutions such as libraries and churches, and Budget Films has made no effort to raise its prices substantially in this area for many years.

Through sound management, some smaller, regional companies have also been able to survive. Minneapolis-based Festival Films was founded in 1975 by film enthusiast Ron Hall, offering a wide variety of 16mm films for sale to collectors and institutions. In 1988, it switched over primarily to videotape sales, specializing in foreign language and classic titles often hard to locate at local video outlets. It continues to offer for sale 16mm prints of Blackhawk releases from Film Preservation Associates, serving as one of the latter's agents as do a number of other distribution outlets, including National Cinema Service and Glenn Photo Supply.

The most expensive videotapes in the Festival Films catalog sell for $89.95 each (*Henry V* [1989], *The Handmaid's Tale* [1990], etc.), while the most expensive 16mm feature films cost more than $500. *The General* (1927) is $750, *The Birth of a Nation* (1915) is $850, *Nights of Cabiria* (1957) is $695, and so on. As a result, from a dollar perspective, 16mm performs reasonably well in comparison with videotape. Since 1988, in dollars, 16mm sales have accounted for 35 percent of Festival's business, and, curiously, for 40 percent in 1991. Hall points out that this figure is a fluke that was caused by unrelated decisions by a number of organizations suddenly to start film collections. One major new client is the Iranian Film Archives, often purchasing two 16mm prints of each title.[9]

Aside from Films Inc., the one 16mm rental house that has thrived and expanded into the 1990s is Kit Parker Films, located in Monterey, California. The company was founded by Parker in 1971 primarily as a library of public domain titles. The first studio to be represented was RKO, followed by Columbia and Walt Disney. Parker has found that his releases of foreign language and classic films, the so-called "art house" titles, continue to rent well to colleges, universities, libraries, and museums that know the company for its "good service and excellent prints," while the rentals of 16mm entertainment titles, primarily to libraries and parks and recreation departments, have declined substantially.[10]

As early as 1981, 16mm rentals began to fall off, and Kit Parker Films began to expand into other areas, including stock footage, from which Parker eventually veered away as too competitive and something he personally hated. Instead, the company began to develop theatrical distribution, beginning in earnest in 1988, and also formed a video division to market its own releases to stores and individuals.

In May 1986, Kit Parker Films made its first major acquisition of a competitor with the takeover of Boston-based Wholesome Film Center, Inc., which had been in existence for some sixty-two years. In 1989, the company purchased Twyman Films, and the following year it acquired Clem Williams Films.

The success of companies such as Kit Parker Films and Films Inc., in the theatrical field led to vague attempts to resurrect 16mm for theatrical exhibition. The assumption was that smaller theatres could just as easily screen 16mm as 35mm. In the 1940s, 16mm theatrical presentations had been advocated, with Paramount requesting that RCA design a 16mm projector for theatrical use in 1940 and the Fox Theatres chain installing a number of 16mm projectors in their auditoriums. There was even a company called 16mm Theatre Circuits of America, Inc., which advocated 16mm theatrical entertainment in the 1948 edition of the *Film World 16mm and Industry Directory*.

In 1989, Larry Jacobson, vice president of American Multi-Cinema, tried to interest exhibitors at the National Association of Theatre Owners (NATO)/ShoWest Seminar in installing 16mm projectors, urging that 16mm prints could be produced at half the cost of 35mm (a correct statement that did not take into account the limited number of laboratories available to make 16mm prints). Jacobson further pointed out that 16mm projection was "indistinguishable" from 35mm in auditoriums with fewer than 400 seats and theatre screens no larger than 17 feet by

34 feet.[11] Despite a demonstration early in 1989 at the AMC theatre complex in Burbank, California, there was negligible interest in the proposal.

Through compromise and change, some non-theatrical companies did survive the video revolution, but most fell by the wayside or became empty shells of their former selves. Their managers might argue that they could not have foreseen what video would do to the non-theatrical medium, but there can be little doubt that the non-theatrical industry paid scant attention to video until it was too late. As Robert Finehout, vice president of Modern Talking Picture Service, wrote in 1981, "The blinding speed with which the video and computer technologies have overtaken—or taken over—communications is like the big-bang theory of creation."[12]

Even Tom Hope of *Hope Reports* was unprepared for the eventual change that video was to wreak on the non-theatrical industry. Writing in *Sponsored Film* in 1976, Walter J. Klein reported,

> So far most videotape production is being done in-house rather than by independent producers. Because of the difference in technology and approach to production, [Tom] Hope envisions most work continuing in the film medium with videotape only taking over that production for which film is not ideally suited in the first place, the recording of a live talk or presentation on a quick basis. "Where a story or plot is used, the film medium is superior to that of tape," according to Hope. "There is a challenge to sponsored film producers to do a better job, possibly using both media. But the capability of making good motion picture prints from videotape at a reasonable cost still does not exist. The 16mm film is the only motion picture medium which can be used any place in the world on anybody's projector."[13]

Much of what Hope stated then is both correct and disputable. For presentation on a television monitor, videotape is superior to film. It is true that it is prohibitively expensive to transfer videotape to film and that the outcome is not aesthetically pleasing, but why bother to make the transfer? Videotape is meant to be viewed on a television monitor, and while standards do vary from country to country, the dubbing (or transfer) from one standard to another is a simple and relatively cheap process.

As early as its first publication, *Hope Reports AV-USA 1969*, Hope's company had made minor reference to videotape. On page 18, under the subject of "Product Categories," the report contains a four-paragraph item on "Videotape Recordings" that notes, "Until there is more hard data (statistics) available from at least three or four VTR libraries, it is not possible to develop a table." In *Hope Reports AV-USA 1971*, tape is given a column in the master table; and in December 1971, Hope Reports published *Motion Pictures and Video Cassettes*. The development of videotape was documented with the August 1975 publication of *Hope Reports Video II*.

As to the first year in which Hope Reports recognized videotape as a threat to the use of film in non-theatrical production, Thomas W. Hope writes, "I would put that year 1975 or 1976. It could even be earlier when we did our first report using video in the title. Take your choice. I lean toward 1971."[14] In 1979, Hope Reports noted that $366.5 million was spent on film production as against $363.7 million for videotape. The following year, it was $400.1 million for videotape and $332.4 million for film.

The non-theatrical film industry's response to videotape was much the same as that of its big theatrical brother. The Hollywood motion picture industry fought the introduction of videotape players and recorders, even going to court to try to stop the American television viewing public from recording programs for later viewing. It was a ridiculous attitude, comparable to that of shortsighted eighteenth-century Englishmen who tried to halt the Industrial Revolution. There is no way to stop progress; one can only hold it in check for a short time and then be swept away by its unrelenting step. Those with foresight use the delaying tactics of others to solidify their positions as users of the new technology.

To embrace video as the non-theatrical film industry had to do meant changing an entire production and distribution set-up. The very machinery that checked the 16mm rental prints was obsolete. The cameras, moviolas, and rewind arms that were the 16mm producer's primary tools were suddenly useless and, more to the point, relatively valueless. To survive, production and distribution companies must purchase new equipment and train new staff. To many, it was a financially worthless endeavor. In many respects, it was easier to establish new companies than try and modify existing organizations. Jerry Fairbanks, whose involvement in industrial and informational film production in Hollywood dated back to the 1930s, was able to retire and rest on his considerable laurels.

Perhaps the company that suffered the most was Eastman Kodak, which had helped the non-theatrical film industry into existence and nurtured it to success (while along the way deriving considerable income from its non-objective concern). As long as the theatrical film industry needs 35mm film, Eastman Kodak will survive, but its 16mm activities are dying and probably will be completely suspended by the end of the twentieth century. Its fate might seem a just reward for a company that doubled the price of its raw stock in 1980 when the cost of silver, an integral part of 16mm and 35mm film, soared but made no appropriate adjustment in its price scheduling when silver values dropped.

Sadly, Eastman Kodak took a long time to come around to reality. It left the production of videotape stock to its competitors from Japan. As late as 1982, Eastman Kodak was taking out advertisements in non-theatrical film journals announcing "FILM: The Imperative. Not the Alternative." The problem was that no one was paying attention.

NOTES

1. Quoted in Daniel Bickley, "Nontheatrical Distribution: The Last Twenty Years," *Sightlines*, vol. XX, no. 1 (Winter 1986/87), p. 15.

2. Quoted in Morry Roth, "16M, 35M Distribs End 40-Year War," *Variety*, September 4, 1974, p. 5.

3. William F. Kruse, "The Feature Film in 16mm," *Film News*, vol. XXIII, no. 4 (1966), p. 7.

4. Quoted in Daniel Bickley, "Nontheatrical Distribution: The Last Twenty Years," *Sightlines*, vol. XX, no. 1 (Winter 1986/87), p. 16.

5. Ibid.

6. *Sightlines*, vol. XXII, no. 3 (Summer 1989), p. 12.

7. Stanley Yates, "The American Archives of the Factual Film," *Sightlines*, vol. XXIV, no. 1 (Winter 1991), p. 15.

8. Daniel J. Perkins, "The Sponsored Film: A New Dimension in American Film Research?" *Historical Journal of Film, Radio and Television*, vol. II, no. 2 (1982), pp. 133–39.

9. Ron Hall in conversation with the author, August 15, 1981.

10. Kit Parker in conversation with the author, August 15, 1981.

11. "Don't Discount 16mm Product," *Daily Variety*, February 17, 1989, pp. 3, 10.

12. Robert Finehout, "Brave New Video World: Is This the Twilight of Film?" *Business & Home TV Screen*, June 26, 1981, p. 45.

13. Walter J. Klein, *Sponsored Film* (New York: Hastings House, 1976), p. 31.

14. Letter from Thomas W. Hope to the author, August 16, 1991.

Appendix A: Major Non-Theatrical Distributors of the 1920s

Alexander Film Corporation
130 West 46th Street
New York, NY

Atlas Educational Film Company
1111 South Boulevard
Oak Park, IL

Austin Film Library, Inc.
Austin, TX

W. J. Benedict
404 Hannah Building
Cleveland, OH

Beseler Educational Film Company, Inc.
71 West 23rd Street
New York, NY

Celebrated Players Film Corporation
810 South Wabash Avenue
Chicago, IL

Central Film Company
729 Seventh Avenue
New York, NY

Clinical Film Libraries
132 West 42nd Street
New York, NY

Community Motion Picture Service, Inc.
46 West 24th Street
New York, NY

Co-operative Film Exchange
107 Golden Gate Avenue
San Francisco, CA

H. O. Davis
125 South Hudson Street
Oklahoma City, OK

Eskay Harris Feature Film Company, Inc.
126–130 West 46th Street
New York, NY

Fine-Art Film Company
738 South Wabash Avenue
Chicago, IL

Geographic Film Company
206 Mercantile Library Building
Cincinnati, OH

Guaranty Pictures Company
130 West 46th Street
New York, NY

Harcol Film Company, Inc.
330 Camp Street
New Orleans, LA

Charles F. Herm, Inc.
220 West 42nd Street
New York, NY

Homestead Films, Inc.
7510 North Ashland Avenue
Chicago, IL

Jawitz Pictures Corporation
729 Seventh Avenue
New York, NY

Albrecht Jensen
P.O. Box 73, General Post Office
New York, NY

Kinema Film Service
806 South Wabash Avenue
Chicago, IL

Lea-Bel Film Company
806 South Wabash Avenue
Chicago, IL

Lewey Studios
853 North Eutaw Street
Baltimore, MD

Matre's Library of Films
76–78 West Lake Street
Chicago, IL

National Non-Theatrical Motion Pictures, Inc.
232 West 38th Street
New York, NY

Picture Service Corporation
729 Seventh Avenue
New York, NY

Plymouth Film Corporation
46 West 24th Street
New York, NY

Queen Feature Service
30–31 Potter Building
Birmingham, AL

Reliable Educational Film Company
6751 East End Avenue
Chicago, IL

Romell Motion Picture Company
115 East 6th Street
Cincinnati, OH

Sanford Film Library
406 Englewood Avenue
Chicago, IL

Southern Enterprises, Inc.
51 Luckie Street
Atlanta, GA

Superior Screen Service, Inc.
738 South Wabash Avenue
Chicago, IL

Temple Pictures, Inc.
736 South Wabash Avenue
Chicago, IL

Temple Producing Corporation
25th and Leigh Streets
Philadelphia, PA

Victor Safety Film Corporation
132 West 42nd Street
New York, NY

Worcester Film Corporation
130 West 46th Street
New York, NY

World Missionary Drama League
17 North State Street
Chicago, IL

Appendix B:
Major Non-Theatrical 16mm
Distributors of the 1930s

Akin and Bagshaw
1425 Williams Street
Denver, CO
(16mm silent and sound)

American Social Hygiene Association
50 West 50th Street
New York, NY
(16mm and 35mm films on venereal disease)

Associated Screen News, Ltd.
Tivoli Theatre Building, 21 Richmond Street East
Toronto, Canada

Bass Camera Company
179 Madison Street
Chicago, IL
(16mm silent and sound)

Bray Pictures Corporation
729 Seventh Avenue
New York, NY
(16mm and 35mm)

Central Camera Company
220 South Wabash Avenue
Chicago, IL

Church and School Film Service
1635 Central Parkway
Cincinnati, OH

Cine Classic Library
1041 Jefferson Avenue
Brooklyn, NY

Cinepix Company
630 Ninth Avenue, Film Center Building
New York, NY

Commonwealth Pictures Corporation
729 Seventh Avenue
New York, NY
(16mm and 35mm)

William M. Dennis
2506½ West 7th Street
Los Angeles, CA

Herman A. DeVry, Inc.
1111 Center Street
Chicago, IL
(16mm and 35mm)

William H. Dudley Visual Education Service, Inc.
736 Wabash Avenue
Chicago, IL
(16mm silent)

Du World Pictures, Inc.
729 Seventh Avenue
New York, NY

Edited Pictures System, Inc.
330 West 42nd Street
New York, NY
(16mm silent and sound)

ERPI Picture Consultants, Inc.
250 West 57th Street
New York, NY

> ERPI instructional sound films also distributed by: University of Kansas,
> Extension Division, Lawrence, Kansas; University of Minnesota, General
> Extension Division, Minneapolis, Minnesota; University of Texas, Extension
> Division, Visual Instruction Bureau, Austin, Texas; University of Wisconsin,
> Bureau of Visual Instruction, Madison, Wisconsin

F.C. Pictures Corporation
505 Pearl Street
Buffalo, NY
(16mm and 35mm)

Films of Commerce Company, Inc.
Pathe Building, 33 West 45th Street

New York, NY
(16mm and 35mm)

Fotoshop Home Movie Rental Library
136 West 32nd Street
New York, NY
(16mm silent)

Garrison Film Distributors, Inc.
729 Seventh Avenue
New York, NY
(16mm sound and 35mm silent and sound)

General Film Library of California
1426 Beachwood Drive
Hollywood, CA

Walter O. Gutlohn, Inc.
33 West 45th Street
New York, NY
(16mm silent and sound)

Harry's Camera Shop
317 West 50th Street
New York, NY

Homestead Films, Inc.
7510 North Ashland Avenue
Chicago, IL

Ideal Pictures Corporation
28 East 8th Street
Chicago, IL
(16mm and 35mm)

Illinois State Department of Public Health
State House
Springfield, IL
("Health and Hygiene Pictures")

Institutional Cinema Service
130 West 46th Street
New York, NY
(16mm silent and sound)

Jewish Talking Picture Company, Inc.
33 West 60th Street
New York, NY

Kinematrade, Inc.
723 Seventh Avenue
New York, NY

F. E. Kleinschmidt
391 Audubon Avenue
New York, NY

Major Film Laboratories, Inc.
120–122 West 41st Street
New York, NY

Manse Film Library
2514 Clifton Avenue
Cincinnati, OH
(16mm silent and sound)

National Motion Picture Service
36 West 55th Street
New York, NY
(16mm and 35mm)

Pinkney Film Service
1028 Forbes Street
Pittsburgh, PA
(16mm and 35mm)

Principal Distributing Corporation
1501 Broadway
New York, NY

Screen Attractions Corporation
630 Ninth Avenue
New York, NY

Southern Film Library
Knoxville, TN

United Projector and Film Corporation
228 Franklin Street
Buffalo, NY

University of Missouri
Visual Education Service
Columbia, MO
(35mm)

Victor Animatograph Corporation
242 West 55th Street
New York, NY

Wholesome Film Service, Inc.
46 Melrose Street
Boston, MA
(16mm and 35mm)

YMCA Motion Picture Bureau
347 Madison Avenue
New York, NY
(16mm and 35mm)

Zenith Camera Service
5011 North Sawyer Avenue
Chicago, IL

Appendix C:
Major Non-Theatrical 16mm
Distributors of the 1940s

Akin and Bagshaw, Inc.
1425 Williams Street
Denver, CO
(16mm silent and sound)

Allen and Allen Productions
6060 Sunset Boulevard
Hollywood, CA
(16mm and 35mm)

Harold Ambrosch
P.O. Box 98
Glendale, CA
(16mm silent and sound)

American Films Foundation, Inc.
2280 Holly Drive
Hollywood, CA
(16mm and 35mm)

American Museum of Natural History
79th Street and Central Park
New York, NY
(16mm silent and sound)

American Social Hygiene Association
50 West 50th Street

New York, NY
(16mm and 35mm)

American Trading Association
723 Seventh Avenue
New York, NY
(16mm and 35mm)

R.B. Annis Company
1101 North Delaware Street
Indianapolis, IN
(16mm silent and sound)

Astor Pictures Corporation
130 West 46th Street
New York, NY

Australia News and Information Bureau
610 Fifth Avenue
New York, NY
(16mm and 35mm)

Bailey Film Service
1651 Cosmo Street
Hollywood, CA
(16mm and 35mm)

Bell & Howell Co.
1801 Larchmont Avenue
Chicago, IL
(16mm silent and sound)
    Branches in Hollywood, New York, and Washington, D.C.

Brandon Films, Inc.
1600 Broadway
New York, NY
(16mm silent and sound)

Bray Pictures Corp.
122 East 42nd Street
New York, NY
(16mm and 35mm)

British Library of Information
30 Rockefeller Plaza
New York, NY
(16mm and 35mm)

Burton Holmes Films, Inc.
7510 Ashland Avenue
Chicago, IL
(16mm silent and sound)

Castle Films
RCA Building
New York, NY

(16mm silent and sound)
    Branches in Chicago and San Francisco

Cathedral Films
Box 589
Hollywood, CA
(16mm sound)

Chicago Film Laboratory, Inc.
18 West Walton Place
Chicago, IL
(16mm and 35mm)

Frank Church Films
6117 Grove Street
Oakland, CA
(16mm and 35mm)

College Film Center
84 East Randolph Street
Chicago, IL
(16mm and 35mm)

Commonwealth Pictures Corp.
729 Seventh Avenue
New York, NY

Davis & Geck
57 Willoughby Street
Brooklyn, NY

D.T. Davis Company
231 West Short Street
Lexington, KY
(16mm silent and sound)

DeFrenes & Company
1909 Buttonwood Street
Philadelphia, PA
(16mm silent)

DeVry Corporation
1111 Armitage Avenue
Chicago, IL
(16mm silent and sound)

Distributor's Group, Inc.
756 West Peachtree Street
Atlanta, GA
(16mm silent and sound)

Film Classic Exchange
505 Pearl Street
Buffalo, NY
(16mm and 35mm)

Films Incorporated
330 West 42nd Street
New York, NY
    Branches in Chicago, Portland, Los Angeles, Austin, and Atlanta

Foster Films
40 East 17th Street
Brooklyn, NY
(16mm silent)

William J. Ganz Co.
19 East 47th Street
New York, NY
(16mm and 35mm)

Garrison Film Distributors, Inc.
1600 Broadway
New York, NY
(16mm and 35mm)

Walter O. Gutlohn, Inc.
25 West 45th Street
New York, NY
(16mm silent and sound)

Harmon Foundation, Inc.
Division of Visual Experiment
140 Nassau Street
New York, NY
(16mm silent and sound)

Hoffberg Productions, Inc.
1600 Broadway
New York, NY
(16mm and 35mm)

Ideal Pictures Corp.
28 East 8th Street
Chicago, IL
(16mm silent and sound)
    Branches in Atlanta, Dallas, Los Angeles, Denver, Memphis, Jacksonville,
    Miami, New York, and Portland

International Film Bureau, Inc.
84 East Randolph Street
Chicago, IL
(16mm and 35mm)

International Harvester Co.
180 North Michigan Avenue
Chicago, IL
(16mm and 35mm)

The Manse Film Library
1521 Dana Avenue

Cincinnati, OH
(16mm silent and sound)

Michigan Film Library
15745 Rosemont Road
Detroit, MI
(16mm and 35mm)

Modern Talking Picture Service
9 Rockefeller Plaza
New York, NY
(16mm and 35mm)

Museum of Modern Art Film Library
11 West 53rd Street
New York, NY
(16mm and 35mm)

National Film Service
National School Supply Co., Inc.
14 Glenwood Avenue
Raleigh, NC
(16mm sound)

Non Theatrical Film Corp.
165 West 46th Street
New York, NY
(16mm silent and sound)

Nu-Art Films, Inc.
145 West 45th Street
New York, NY
(16mm and 35mm)

Official Films, Inc.
425 Fourth Avenue
New York, NY
(16mm and 35mm)

Photo & Sound, Inc.
153 Kearny Street
San Francisco, CA

Post Pictures Corp.
723 Seventh Avenue
New York, NY
(16mm and 35mm)

Ray-Bell Films, Inc.
2269 Ford Parkway
St. Paul, MN
(16mm and 35mm)

Southern Visual Equipment Co.
492 South Second Street
Memphis, TN

Swank Motion Pictures
620 North Skinker Boulevard
St. Louis, MO
(16mm silent and sound)

Visual Art Films Distributors
204 Empire Building
Pittsburgh, PA

Visual Education Service
131 Clarendon Street
Boston, MA
(16mm silent and sound)

Wholesome Film Service, Inc.
48 Melrose Street
Boston, MA
(16mm and 35mm)

Yale University Press Film Service
386 Fourth Avenue
New York, NY
(16mm and 35mm)

Appendix D:
Useful Non-Theatrical Addresses

American Film & Video Association
920 Barnsdale Road, Suite 152
La Grange Park, IL 60525

American Film & Video Festival
920 Barnsdale Road, Suite 152
La Grange Park, IL 60525

Ann Arbor Film Festival
Box 8232
Ann Arbor, MI 48107

Association of Visual Communicators
7440 North Figueroa Street, Suite 103
Los Angeles, CA 90041

Back Stage
330 West 42nd Street
New York, NY 10036

Birmingham International Educational Film Festival
Box 2641
Birmingham, AL 35291–0665

Budget Films, Inc.
4590 Santa Monica Boulevard
Los Angeles, CA 90029

Canyon Cinema, Inc.
2325 Third Street, Suite 338
San Francisco, CA 94107

Carousel Films, Inc.
260 Fifth Ave, Room 705
New York, NY 10001

Catholic Audio-Visual Educators
1000 McNeally Road
Pittsburgh, PA 15226

Churchill Films
12210 Nebraska Avenue
Los Angeles, CA 90025

The Cinema Guild
1697 Broadway, Room 802
New York, NY 10019

Columbus International Film and Video Festival
1229 Third Avenue
Columbus, OH 45212

Coronet/MTI Film & Video
108 Wilmot Road
Deerfield, IL 60015

Council on International Nontheatrical Events
1001 Connecticut Avenue, N.W., Suite 1016
Washington, DC 20036

Dance Film Association, Inc.
1133 Broadway, Room 507
New York, NY 10010

Direct Cinema Ltd.
Box 69799
Los Angeles, CA 90069

Em Gee Film Library
6924 Canby Avenue, Suite 103
Reseda, CA 91335

Encyclopaedia Britannica Educational Corp.
310 South Michigan Avenue
Chicago, IL 60604

Film Council of Greater Columbus
1229 West Third Avenue
Columbus, OH 43212

Film-Makers' Cooperative
175 Lexington Avenue
New York, NY 10016

Films for the Humanities, Inc.
743 Alexander Road
Princeton, NJ 08540

Films Inc.
5547 North Ravenswood Avenue
Chicago, IL 60640

Griggs-Moviedrome
263 Harrison Street
Nutley, NJ 07110

Hope Reports, Inc.
1600 Lyell Avenue
Rochester, NY 14606

International Documentary Association
1551 South Robertson Boulevard, Suite 201
Los Angeles, CA 90035

Ivy Films
165 West 46th Street
New York, NY 10036

Landers Film & Video Reviews
Box 27309
Escondido, CA 92027

Media & Methods
1429 Walnut Street
Philadelphia, PA 19102

Modern Talking Picture Service, Inc.
5000 Park Street North
St. Petersburg, FL 33709

National Audiovisual Center
  of the National Archives and Records Service
8700 Edgeworth Drive
Capitol Heights, MD 20743

New Day Films
121 West 27th Street, Room 902
New York, NY 10001

New York Film/Video Council
Box 1685
New York, NY 10185

Kit Parker Films, Inc.
1245 10th Street
Monterey, CA 93940

Pathescope Educational Media, Inc.
90 South Bedford Road
Mount Kisco, NY 10549

Professional Audio-Visual Retailers Association
9140 Ward Parkway
Kansas City, MO 64114

Pyramid Films & Video
Box 1048
Santa Monica, CA 90406

Sightlines
920 Barnsdale Road, Suite 152
La Grange Park, IL 60525

Society for Visual Education, Inc.
1345 Diversey Parkway
Chicago, IL 60614

Swank Motion Pictures, Inc.
211 South Jefferson Street
St. Louis, MO 63103

Teaching Films, Inc.
930 Pitner Avenue
Evanston, IL 60202

University Film & Video Association
100 Beacon Street
Boston, MA 02116

World Wide Pictures, Inc.
1201 Hennepin Avenue
Minneapolis, MN 55403

Zipporah Films, Inc.
1 Richdale Avenue, Unit 4
Cambridge, MA 02140

Selected Bibliography

Ackerman, Carl. *George Eastman*. Boston: Houghton Mifflin, 1930.

"Agriculture on Film." *Film News*, vol. XIX, no. 5 (November-December 1952), pp. 6–7, 23.

" 'Angel with a Camera in His Arms' Brings Bob Jones' Films to World Audience," *Business Screen*, vol. XXII, no. 2 (April 28, 1961), p. 42.

Behlmer, Rudy. "Land of Liberty a Conglomerate." *American Cinematographer*, vol. LXXII, no. 3 (March 1991), pp. 34–40.

Bickley, Daniel. "Nontheatrical Distribution: The Last Twenty Years." *Sightlines*, vol. XX, no. 1 (Winter 1986/87), pp. 14–18.

Brantu, John W. "Rural America and the Screen." *Business Screen*, vol. VIII, no. 7 (November 1947), pp. 23–24.

Brooker, Floyd E. "Motion Pictures as an Aid to Education." *The Annals of the American Academy of Political and Social Science*, 1947, pp. 103–9.

Burder, John W. *The Work of the Industrial Film Maker*. New York: Communication Arts Books, 1973.

Burt, F. Allen. *American Advertising Agencies: An Inquiry into Their Origins, Growth, Functions and Future*. New York: Harper & Brothers, 1940.

Cocks, Orrin G. "Libraries and Motion Pictures—An Ignored Educational Agency." *Library Journal*, vol. XIX, no. 9 (September 1914), pp. 666–69.

Collins, Douglas. *The Story of Kodak*. New York: Harry N. Abrams, 1990.

"Conference on 8mm Sound Film and Education." *Film News*, vol. XIX, no. 1 (January-February 1962), pp. 6–15.

Cox, George L. "The Industrial Film—Yesterday and To-Day." *New York Dramatic Mirror*, April 15, 1914, p. 36.

Daniel, Hawthorne. "American History in Moving Pictures." *The World's Work*, September 1922, pp. 540–47.

Dewey, Melvil. "Our Next Half Century." *Library Journal*, vol. LI, no. 18 (October 15, 1926), pp. 887–89.

De Witt, Jack. *Producing Industrial Films: From Fade-In to Fade-Out*. South Brunswick, N.J.: A.S. Barnes, 1968.

Doyle, R. E. "50 Years of Films." *Business Screen*, vol. XXX, no. 8 (August 1969), p. 32.

Ehlinger, Cliff. "Video and Film Libraries Herald a New Era." *Sightlines*, vol. XXII, no. 1 (Winter 1988/89), p. 14.

Ellis, Don Carlos, and Laura Thornborough. *Motion Pictures in Education*. New York: Thomas Crowell, 1923.

Evans, Raymond. "The Motion Picture Policy of the United States Department of Agriculture." *Educational Screen*, vol. XVI, no. 9 (November 1937), pp. 283–85.

"Farm Film Foundation Gains Stature." *Business Screen*, vol. XI, no. 4 (June 26, 1950), p. 31.

"The Film in Medicine." *Business Screen*, vol. XIII, no. 6 (September 28, 1952), pp. 27–29.

Finehout, Robert. "Sponsored Film: Talking Pictures to Satellite Transmission." *Business & Home TV Screen*, November 1978, pp. 18–19.

———. "Brave New Video World: Is This the Twilight of Film?" *Business & Home TV Screen*, June 26, 1981, pp. 44–47.

Flory, John. "The Challenge of 8mm Sound Film." *Educational Screen & Audio-Visual Guide*, vol. XXXX, no. 7 (July 1961), pp. 334–35.

Freeman, Frank N., ed. *Visual Education: A Comparative Study of Motion Pictures and Other Methods of Instruction*. Chicago: University of Chicago Press, 1924.

Gingrich, Arnold. *Nothing But People: The Early Days at Esquire, A Personal History, 1928–1958*. New York: Crown, 1971.

Gordon, Jay E. *Motion Picture Production for Industry*. New York: Macmillan, 1961.

Grierson, John. "Non-Theatrical Revolution." *Film News*, vol. V, no. 9 (November 1944), pp. 4–5.

Hamilton, Clayton. "American History on the Screen." *The World's Work*, September 1924, pp. 525–32.

Herman, Lewis. *Educational Films: Writing, Direction and Producing for Classroom, Television and Industry*. New York: Crown, 1965.

Jacob, Livio, and Russell Merritt. "The Night I Saw Traffic in Souls: An Interview with David Shepard." *Griffithiana*, no. 38/39 (October 1990), pp. 227–34.

Jacobs, Dr. Sarnoff. "The Cinema in Surgery." *Educational Screen*, vol. XIV, no. 1 (January 1935), pp. 9–10, 22–23.

"Jamison Handy—Founder of Business Audiovisuals." *Business Screen*, vol. XXXII, no. 2 (February 1971), pp. 33–35; vol. XXXII, no. 3 (March 1971), pp. 23–24.

Jones, Emily S. "Remembering EFLA: 1945–1958." *Sightlines*, vol. XVII, nos. 1/2 (Fall/Winter 1983/84), pp. 6–8.

———. "In the Beginning: Sightlines." *Sightlines*, vol. XX, no. 2 (Winter 1986/87), p. 4.

Klein, Walter J. *Sponsored Film*. New York: Hastings House, 1976.
"Kodak's 16mm History—From Lab to World Use." *Film News*, vol. VIII, no. 12 (June-July 1948), pp. 7–8.
Kogan, Herman. *The Great EB: The Story of the Encyclopaedia Britannica*. Chicago: University of Chicago Press, 1958.
Krahn, Federic A. "Index to Articles on Films in Public Libraries." *Film News*, vol. XXIV, no. 5 (1967), pp. 17–19.
Krows, Arthur Edwin. "A Quarter Century of Non-Theatrical Films." *Educational Screen*, vol. XV, no. 6 (June 1936), pp. 169–73.
———. "Motion Pictures—Not for Theatres," *Educational Screen*, vol. XVII, no. 7 (September 1938), pp. 211–15; vol. XVII, no. 8 (October 1938), pp. 249–53; vol. XVII, no. 9 (November 1938), pp. 291–94; vol. XVII, no. 10 (December 1938), pp. 325–28; vol. XVIII, no. 1 (January 1939), pp. 13–16; vol. XVIII, no. 2 (February 1939), pp. 49–51; vol. XVIII, no. 3 (March 1939), pp. 85–88; vol. XVIII, no. 4 (April 1939), pp. 121–24; vol. XVIII, no. 5 (May 1939), pp. 153–56; vol. XVIII, no. 6 (June 1939), pp. 191–94, 208; vol. XVIII, no. 7 (September 1939), pp. 242–45; vol. XVIII, no. 8 (October 1939), pp. 284–88; vol. XVIII, no. 9 (November 1939), pp. 329–32, 349; vol. XVIII, no. 10 (December 1939), pp. 362–65; vol. XIX, no. 1 (January 1940), pp. 16–18; vol. XIX, no. 2 (February 1940), pp. 58–61; vol. XIX, no. 5 (May 1940), pp. 193–97; vol. XIX, no. 6 (June 1940), pp. 235–38, 242; vol. XIX, no. 7 (September 1940), pp. 286–89; vol. XIX, no. 8 (October 1940), pp. 333–36; vol. XIX, no. 9 (November 1940), pp. 379–81, 402; vol. XIX, no. 10 (December 1940), pp. 417–19; vol. XX, no. 1 (January 1941), pp. 15–17, 42; vol. XX, no. 2 (February 1941), pp. 61–64; vol. XX, no. 3 (March 1941), pp. 107–9; vol. XX, no. 4 (April 1941), pp. 150–52; vol. XX, no. 5 (May 1941), pp. 198–200, 223; vol. XX, no. 6 (June 1941), pp. 241–42; vol. XX, no. 7 (September 1941), pp. 284–85, 292; vol. XX, no. 8 (October 1941), pp. 333–35; vol. XX, no. 9 (November 1941), pp. 383–85; vol. XX, no. 10 (December 1941), pp. 427–29; vol. XXI, no. 1 (January 1941), pp. 14–17, 21; vol. XXI, no. 2 (February 1942), pp. 61–63; vol. XXI, no. 3 (March 1942), pp. 104–6; vol. XXI, no. 4 (April 1942), pp. 138–40; vol. XXI, no. 5 (May 1942), pp. 180–82; vol. XXI, no. 6 (June 1942), pp. 222–23, 242; vol. XXI, no. 7 (September 1942), pp. 259–61, 264; vol. XXI, no. 8 (October 1942), pp. 302–4, 306; vol. XXI, no. 9 (November 1942), pp. 348–50; vol. XXI, no. 10 (December 1942), pp. 386–87, 404; vol. XXII, no. 1 (January 1943), pp. 14–16; vol. XXII, no. 2 (February 1943), pp. 53–55, 79; vol. XXII, no. 3 (March 1943), pp. 94–96, 119; vol. XXII, no. 4 (April 1943), pp. 133–35; vol. XXII, no. 5 (May 1943), pp. 170–72, 190; vol. XXII, no. 6 (June 1943), pp. 206–8, 219; vol. XXII, no. 7 (September 1943), pp. 243–46; vol. XXII, no. 8 (October 1943), pp. 295–97, 319; vol. XXII, no. 9 (November 1943), pp. 358–40; vol. XXII, no. 10 (December 1943), pp. 383–85; vol. XXIII, no. 1 (January 1944), pp. 19–22; vol. XXIII, no. 2 (February 1944), pp. 69–71; vol. XXIII, no. 3 (March 1944), pp. 115–17, 142; vol. XXIII, no. 4 (April 1944), pp. 161–63; vol. XXIII, no. 5 (May 1944), pp. 207–9; vol. XXIII, no. 6 (June 1944), pp. 248–50.
Kruse, William F. "... Not Born Yesterday." *Educational Screen & Audio-Visual Guide*, vol. XXXVIII, no. 2 (February 1959), pp. 76–78.

Larson, L. C. "The Formation of the Educational Film Library Association." *Film News*, vol. IV, no. 1 (Summer 1943), pp. 11–12.

Lewin, William. "Teachers Hail the Talkies." *Educational Screen*, vol. VIII, no. 10 (December 1929), p. 295.

Lipton, Lenny. *The Super 8 Book*. San Francisco: Straight Arrow Books, 1975.

McClusky, F. Dean. "A-V 1905–1955." *Educational Screen*, vol. XXXIV, no. 4 (April 1955), pp. 160–62.

McDonald, Gerald Doan. *Educational Motion Pictures and Libraries*. Chicago: American Library Association, 1942.

MacEachern, Malcolm T. "War Medicine and the Screen." *Business Screen*, vol. IV, no. 2 (March 1, 1942), pp. 14, 27.

McGuire, Jerry. *How to Write, Direct & Produce Effective Business Films & Documentaries*. Blue Ridge Summit, Pa.: TAB, 1978.

McKee, Gerald. *Classic Home Movie Projectors: 1922–1940*. Gerrards Cross, United Kingdom: The Author, 1989.

Mayer, Harold M. and Richard C. Wade. *Chicago: Growth of a Metropolis*. Chicago: University of Chicago Press, 1969.

Mercer, John. *The Informational Film*. Champaign, Ill.: Stipes Publishing Company, 1981.

Montague, J. F. *Taking the Doctor's Pulse*. Philadelphia: J.B. Lippincott, 1928.

"The Motion Picture as a 'Handmaid of Religion.' " *Literary Digest*, vol. LXV, no. 7 (May 15, 1920), pp. 46–47.

Nichtenhauser, Adolf, Marie L. Coleman, and David S. Ruhe. *Films in Psychiatry, Psychology & Mental Health*. New York: Health Education Council, 1953.

"Orton Hicks Reminisces." *Film News*, vol. VIII, no. 12 (June-July 1948), pp. 10, 26.

Perkins, Daniel J. "The Sponsored Film: A New Dimension in American Film Research?" *Historical Journal of Film, Radio and Television*, vol. II, no. 2 (1982), pp. 133–39.

―――. "Sponsored Business Films: An Overview 1895–1955." *Film Reader*, no. 6 (1985), pp. 125–32.

Peyton, Patricia, ed. *Reel Change: Guide to Social Issue Films*. San Francisco and New York: The Film Fund, 1979.

Pierce, David. "Silent Movies and the Kodascope Libraries." *American Cinematographer*, vol. LXX, no. 1 (January 1989), pp. 34–39.

Prelinger, Richard, and Celeste R. Hoffnar, eds. *Footage 89*. New York: Prelinger Associates, 1989.

Ramsaye, Terry. "The Picture and Education." *Educational Screen*, vol. IX, no. 6 (May 1930), pp. 134–36.

Robinson, Jack Fay. *Bell & Howell Company: A 75-Year History*. Chicago: Bell & Howell Company, 1982.

Rose, Samuel G. "Alexander F. Victor—Motion Picture Pioneer." *Journal of the SMPTE*, vol. LXXII, no. 8 (August 1963), pp. 614–21.

Roth, Morry. "16M, 35M Distribs End 40-Year War." *Variety*, September 4, 1974, p. 5.

Schreiber, Flora Rheta. "New York—A Cinema Capital." *Quarterly of Film, Radio and Television*, vol. VII, no. 3 (Spring 1953), pp. 264–73.

Sewell, George H. *Commercial Cinematography*. London: Sir Isaac Pitman & Sons, n.d.

Shepard, David H. *Victor Animatograph Company and the Genesis of Non-Theatrical Film*. Privately published, 1985.

"16mm Finds Its Voice." *Film News*, vol. VIII, no. 12 (June-July 1948), p. 9.

Slade, Mark. "Eight Millimeter: The Eighth Lively Art." *Educational Screen & Audio-Visual Guide*, vol. XXXXI, No. 10 (July-October 1962), pp. 598–99.

Slide, Anthony. "Kent D. Eastin." *Films in Review*, vol. XXXII, no. 7 (August/September 1981), pp. 435, 441.

Smith, Roy L. *Moving Pictures in the Church*. New York: Abingdon Press, 1921.

"Sound Films Go to School." *Film News*, vol. VIII, no. 12 (June-July 1948), p. 13.

"A Specialist in a Fine Art." *Photoplay*, vol. XV, no. 1 (December 1918), pp. 57–58.

"This Is the Modern Story. . . ." *Business Screen*, vol. XIX, no. 2 (March 30, 1958), pp. 36–37; vol. XIX, no. 3 (May 15, 1958), pp. 38, 64; vol. XIX, no. 4 (June 15, 1958), pp. 44–45, 64.

Thomas, Edwin J. "Chicago Is Not an Island." *Educational Screen*, vol. XXII, no. 10 (December 1944), pp. 429–32.

"Through the Portals—The Story of Bray Studios, Inc." *Film News*, vol. VIII, no. 12 (June-July 1948), pp. 11, 26.

Trachtenberg, Leo. *The Sponsor's Guide to Filmmaking*. New York: Hopkinson and Blake, 1978.

Vogel, Amos. "Cinema 16 Explained." *Film News*, vol. VIII, no. 10 (March-April 1948), p. 19.

Waldron, Gloria. *The Information Film*. New York: Columbia University Press, 1949.

Weber, Joseph J. "A Selected and Partially Annotated Bibliography on the Use of Visual Aids in Education." *Educational Screen*, vol. IV, no. 9 (November 1925), pp. 573–76.

"Willard Cook: Father of Non-Theatrical in the U.S.A." *Film News*, vol. VIII, no. 12 (June-July 1948), pp. 5, 8.

Wilson, William H., and Kenneth B. Haas. *Film Book: For Business, Education and Industry*. Englewood Cliffs, N.J.: Prentice-Hall, 1951.

"Yale's Movie Version of American History." *Literary Digest*, vol. LXXII, no. 9 (March 4, 1922), pp. 39–40, 43.

Yates, Stanley. "The American Archives of the Factual Film" *Sightlines*, vol. XXIV, no. 1 (Winter 1991), pp. 15–16.

Index

About the Author

ANTHONY SLIDE has held executive positions with both the American Film Institute and the Academy of Motion Picture Arts and Sciences. He is the author or editor of more than forty books on the history of popular entertainment, including *Sourcebook for the Performing Arts* (with Patricia King and Stephen L. Hanson, Greenwood, 1988), *The International Film Industry* (Greenwood, 1989), and *The Television Industry* (Greenwood, 1991). Slide has also been active in the 16mm field. He has directed three short documentaries on Hollywood film personalities and in 1991 completed a feature length documentary, *The Silent Feminists: America's First Women Directors*. Just as *Before Video* is a pioneering, first history of the non-theatrical film, Slide has also authored first-time histories of *Early American Cinema*, *Early Women Directors*, and *The Cinema and Ireland*.

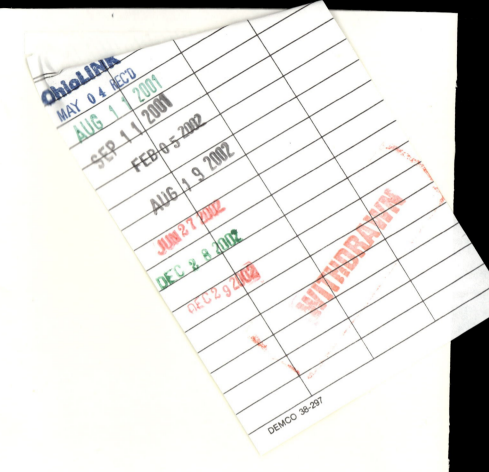